“Every woman reading this can find
‘the strong power’ within to be lived ... God intended. This book is an ‘Unleashing Moment’ for the Church of the 21st Century.”

—Jo Anne Lyon
General Superintendent
The Wesleyan Church

“*[Reclaiming Eve]* is a grand and powerful story of God’s plan—for women in his kingdom, for an amazing alliance between his sons and daughters, for living out the redemption and restoration purchased by Jesus. Suzanne, Carla, and Jamie have woven together their stories and the stories of other *ezers* to portray what can happen when God’s children live out who God made them to be, working together to do the kingdom work he has given them.”

—Judy Douglass
Director of Women’s Resources, Cru Board member,
Synergy Women’s Network, Redbud Writers Guild

“Women at every stage of life will gain valuable perspective and practical ways to reclaim their identity in Christ. Whether you’re looking for a book to read individually or one you can discuss with a group, *Reclaiming Eve* stirs up great food for reflection and discussion.”

—Marian V. Liautaud, editor, *Today’s Christian Woman*
Author, *The War on Women: The World’s Worst Holocaust, and How Christians Are Saving One Girl at a Time*

“With cohesive thinking and scriptural exposition, Burden, Sunberg, and Wright lay out a compelling and exhilarating picture of God’s best for women in a world and church that have limited and undercut the fullness of what God first intended. This is a book about wholeness and freedom in a broken and constrained world. God has created us all—men and women—to walk in balanced wholeness. And he has provided the fullness of the gospel to allow us to restore the imbalance. This insightful read helps women to embrace their identity and both women and men to live as equals who complement one another.”

—Kevin Mannoia
Azusa Pacific University,
Founder, Wesleyan Holiness Consortium

"This is a refreshing look at God's original intentions for all his daughters. It provides a fascinating journey into the meaning of the first words in scripture used to describe God's purpose for women. As *ezers*, we are strong and powerful, created to be God's reflection in the world. This book will counter any residual belief that women are to sit quietly by watching others serve."

—Aletha Hinthorn
Director of "Come to the Fire,"
Founder of Women Alive! Ministries

"Kudos to Burden, Sunberg, and Wright for giving us their special gifts of insight into the role of women and their own self-understanding in our contemporary world. They bring to the task a wide range of experience, a strong faith in the gospel, and in-depth biblical study. Then they deftly use specific illustrations of the implications and applications of the truths they have discovered. The memorable use of the Hebrew word for 'helper' coupled with 'image-bearer' language sets the stage for a solid contribution to understanding and practice."

—Dr. Morris Weigelt
Professor Emeritus of New Testament and Spiritual Formation,
Nazarene Theological Seminary

"I thoroughly enjoyed reading *Reclaiming Eve* and wish it could have been available earlier in my life. This book definitely inspires women to confidently and biblically allow God to 'unfreeze' them in reclaiming their identity as women created and restored in God's image, and to rest in God's plan for their lives and ministry."

—Dr. Nina Gunter
General Superintendent Emeritus,
Church of the Nazarene

"While reading *Reclaiming Eve*, there were many times when I wished I had the opportunity to sit around a table with the three authors discussing the 'hot topics' they addressed. . . . The authors don't shy away from any of the controversial issues that continue to surround the debate over women's identity, role, or calling. They ground their perspective in a solid biblical framework with plentiful references to the Holy Spirit. *Reclaiming Eve* is a valuable reference for understanding the equality God intends for men and women."

—Rev. Dr. Susie C. Stanley
Founder and Executive Director,
Wesleyan/Holiness Women Clergy, Intl. 1991-2006

RECLAIMING EVE

The Identity & Calling of Women in the Kingdom of God

SUZANNE BURDEN
CARLA SUNBERG
JAMIE WRIGHT

BEACON HILL PRESS
OF KANSAS CITY

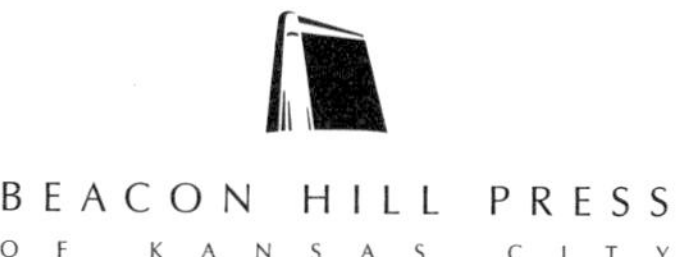

ISBN 978-0-8341-3226-9

Printed in the
United States of America

Cover Design: Jacque Cork
Interior Design: Sharon Page

Library of Congress Control Number: 2013949094

10 9 8 7 6 5 4 3 2 1

CONTENTS

ACKNOWLEDGMENTS

For our mothers, our sisters, and our daughters

Suzanne:

Along the way, I believe hundreds of hearts have touched this project. Thank you to my husband who believed in me and in it before I did, persistently paving the way for its publication when I wanted to give up. Thank you to every other male who has pushed me to engage in the alliance God intended. You are a rousing chorus! Thank you to Carolyn Custis James, the first theologian I read who showed me my identity as a woman did not depend on my circumstances, but on my identity in Christ. This book would not be possible without her scholarship. Thank you to seminary and life buds, Brooke and Natasha, who continuously teach me the power of women believing in one another. My fond appreciation goes to those who have shaped my thinking in theological conversations, and to the friends who allowed part of their stories to be shared here. And thank you to my coauthors: talented, Jesus-loving women who long to see God's kingdom come on earth as it is in heaven. I pray I never stop learning from you.

Jamie:

This is for all my grandmas, aunts, mothers, and sisters—biological and spiritual—who have faithfully shown me what it is to be a woman of God. Thank you particularly to my mom and dad for all usual stuff, particularly the many late-night theological debates throughout the years. Thank you to those who allowed me to use their stories. Thanks to my husband, Ryan, a "liberator of women," for being generous, honest, and affirming through this whole process, and to Toby for being a darling little goober. Most of all, all praise and glory to Christ for the wonderful work he did in each of us while bringing this project about, and for making sure I couldn't weasel my way out of it.

Carla:
Marie Johnson, my grandmother, was a woman who was locked into a small space by the barriers placed upon her by society and the church. While she has already gone to be with Jesus, she is an inspiration and I hope that in some small measure, this book sets her free. That baton of freedom within the kingdom is passed along to my daughters, Christy and Cara, incredible women of God who are now given the opportunity live out the passions of their great-grandmother. My mother, Alice Johnson, is found often within these pages and continues to be my role model. Our "Champion" along the way has been my dear husband Chuck. Without his prodding this project would never have begun. A special thanks to Suzanne and Jamie for joining me in this journey as we helped one another wrestle with the ideas found within these pages.

INTRODUCTION

WHY START FROM THE VERY BEGINNING?

Sixty-two-year-old Nancy glances around the church she's attended for thirty years, fearful someone will realize she's not a godly matriarch, but a fraud. Her husband thinks she's happy in her marriage and satisfied with serving in the nursery twice a month, but Nancy's asking: *Who am I? And am I too old to ask?*

Rachelle is nineteen and wondering: *What is God's plan for me as a woman?* So far she hasn't found any answers in the Bible—it looks like she'll have to figure things out on her own.

Divorced for six months, thirty-five-year-old Jodi's bank account has run dry. At least her new job challenges her to grow—but she's still wondering if she can find healing and restoration in her church. And more than anything, her heart asks: *What does God think of me?*

Every daughter of Eve faces an identity crisis at some time in her life. And many of us wonder on a regular basis where we fit in. For the women who follow Christ, they rightly believe God's Word will hold the answers. But what about those seasons in life when we don't fit the typical mold? Does God have a plan for us then? And what might the first woman he created, Eve, tell us about our true identity? Might she hold the clues to how God sees us and where he wants us to make a difference in his world? We believe so—and that's why we're conducting our identity search at the very beginning, with the very first woman.

IT'S NOT EASY BEING EVE

We, the multigenerational women writing this book, have assembled a list of the roles we've played in life: daughter, sister, wife, mother, friend, church leader, homemaker, writer, missionary, nurse, student, teacher, counselor, evangelist, and the list goes on. Add your many roles to the list. A woman can be and is many things to many people. Probably too many things, as we often feel pulled and stretched beyond the twenty-four hours each day holds.

Maybe you've never thought much about why many of us—probably most of us—feel so fragmented, so not *enough*, so tired. Shouldn't we be happier, more fulfilled? Shouldn't we feel more . . . competent? After all, so many work and ministry opportunities are opening to us, so many modern conveniences are available for us to consume, and so many resources are available for self-improvement. Why in the world is it so taxing to be a daughter of Eve?

The way we see it, we're getting two competing messages that threaten to destroy the beauty of God's image displayed through his daughters:

The World. Part of the message of the feminist movement of the sixties and seventies was that we should leave home to get a job, where we would become infinitely more fulfilled. And while we've pushed and struggled to break the glass ceiling—and much of this has brought wonderful gains for women—we've sadly missed the mark. A woman's place should be valued, whether it is at home or in the public sphere.

Perhaps saddest of all is the power women now feel pressured to wield through their sexuality. Author Lilian Calles Barger put it this way: "Sexually liberated, we seize opportunities to use physical attraction to get the power we still lack . . . we find ourselves material girls forever rooted to the mirror."[1] And University of Michigan professor Susan Douglas lamented, "True power . . . has to do with getting men to lust after you and other women to envy you."[2]

Ouch.

Face-lift, tummy tuck, revealing clothes—striving to be sexier and more desirable consumes the average female. It's as if a smaller waist size and better highlights will give us the power and significance we long for. Even the most modest among us are self-conscious. Every daughter of Eve wants to be noticed and celebrated—in return, we get a mound of insecurity and the feeling that no matter what we give up to be more desirable, it's never enough.

The Church. Surely we can discover who we are in God's house, right? The church has been the source of spiritual healing and wholeness for many women—a place where we experience and live out the hope of the gospel in a hurting world. But, for others, it's become a place where we are often viewed with suspicion and not always given an opportunity to use our voices or our spiritual gifts.

We read the Gospels and marvel at how Jesus exalted the role of women, teaching women alongside his male disciples. Yet we shake our heads, as key figures in church history have painted our grandmother Eve primarily as a temptress rather than God's image-bearer. Our church father Augustine went even farther, insisting a woman didn't bear the image of God until she married.[3] He was clearly wrong, according to Scripture. But that hasn't stopped this flawed impression from seeping into the minds of the very people God wants to use to advance his kingdom.

Something is broken, isn't it? And you and I long for it to be fixed, to be made right again.

GOD'S WORD OFFERS HOPE FOR WOMEN OF EVERY AGE

We've got good news for you! The key to women assuming their rightful place in the world—and in God's kingdom—is not far away. It's tucked into the pages of a Bible near you. And we believe that what you find there, detailed in the pages that follow, will amaze you. It certainly surprised and delighted us . . . and we've been sitting in the church pew all our lives.

A few years ago, we (Carla, Suzanne, and Jamie) set out to find out what the Bible says about every woman's identity. What we uncovered led to prayer, tears, laughter, and finally, a women's Bible study. As we dug into God's Word, women of every stage in life were set free to become all they can be in God's kingdom, and our own hearts soared with joy and relief.

You see, tucked carefully into the creation story is the key to every woman's purpose, from a two-day-old infant to a ninety-year-old great-grandmother:

> *The* L*ORD God said, "It is not good for the man* [adam] *to be alone. I will make a helper* [ezer] *suitable for him."* (Genesis 2:18)

God will make a what? *Ezer* (pronounced *ay´ zer*) is the Hebrew word used when the Bible was first written—the word God used to indicate Eve's soul-DNA, her very reason for being. Although most translations call it "helper" in English, our English word is hardly adequate to describe the depth of God's original intentions for all his daughters. In fact, because we haven't dug deeper to find out more, we have often lost our way.

We'll start with investigating the ways you as an "ezer" are a strong power and agent of rescue. We'll dive into God's intentions for men and women to form a blessed, fruitful alliance at home and at work and in church. And we'll learn what it looks like to be "ezers" who not only grow to be all we can be in Christ but also make a difference in the world by carrying the image and love of Christ to those who need it most.

Throughout this book, we'll use the words "ezer," "strong helper," and "strong power" interchangeably. We'll dive into these meanings in-depth in the next chapter.

So thank you, dear reader, for picking up this book. We've much to discover about our Creator and his plans for each of his female image-bearers. So without further delay, let's begin *Reclaiming Eve*. Won't you join us?

1

The L*ORD* *God said, "It is not good for the man* [adam] *to be alone. I will make a helper* [ezer] *suitable for him."* (Genesis 2:18)

IDENTITY

CREATED IN THE IMAGE OF GOD

"I read that Adam and Eve story in Genesis," she said, shaking her head. "And what happened with Eve was not cool." I had to agree with my young friend Ann, who had recently started reading the Bible. As I (Suzanne) looked into her eyes, I saw reflections of my own heartbreaking disappointment with Eve. *Good grief—I've never met the woman, but she follows me everywhere.*

For pinned on her shoulders, tied to her sorry reputation, and sealed with all the force of hardened cement, remain our perceptions of the woman who was first deceived. Put bluntly, I've come to believe that our thoughts about Eve in general ain't pretty. And who could blame us? Her deception led to our tendency to be deceived. Her sin birthed our sin. Her selfishness ushered daily pain into our lives. We have pain in childbirth and broken relationships to thank her for, misunderstandings and outright evil and injustice, not to mention the daily grind of trying to follow God in a world gone wrong.

And it all started with Eve . . . or so we've been told. (Not that we would have done any differently, if given the choice.) But still. The nicest thing we might say about Eve is that in every Bible story book we've ever read, she has great hair! But as everyone knows: those pictures don't count for anything.

So that leaves us with nothing. Absolutely nothing good to say about Eve. Or does it?

For years, I nursed a secret grudge against Eve. I don't remember talking about it openly, and I'm not sure I admitted it even to myself, but I had serious Eve issues. Some of them were almost comical; others were downright disastrous. Only in the last few years have I begun to realize where my thoughts on Eve went wrong.

As a single woman who longed for a godly husband, I suppose I first resented the fact that Eve didn't have to use an online dating site to find Adam. I envied the absolute assuredness that they were made for each other. *Bone of my bone, flesh of my flesh. Sigh.* Simmering beneath the surface was also the ugly fear that as an unmarried woman I didn't measure up to God's ideal. Forget about having kids as my biological clock ticked on: since I couldn't even find the right Adam, I often felt I hadn't even passed *Womanhood 101*.

Then there was Eve's obvious gullibility factor. All Satan had to do was ask her a question, "Did God really say?" and she was a goner. Never mind the fact that the account in Genesis 3 may have recorded the conversation when it was already halfway through. Or that Adam, too, willingly ate the fruit. I got the impression that Eve was easy prey, making her—and every woman after her—seem somehow inferior.

Finally, my grudge culminated in an outright anger over the effects of sin the first couple ushered in. "Your desire will be for your husband, and he will rule over you" (Genesis 3:16). At the time, the desire for a husband seemed like it would be an outright blessing, rather than a curse. But the "rule over you" part made me feel somehow subservient to every man with whom I came in contact.

I never really brought up my Eve issues in polite conversation. I didn't exactly hear them covered in a Sunday sermon. And I never managed to bring the specifics to the surface in my counselor's office.

Yet Eve and the issues she raised in my heart were there, following me wherever I went. These issues caused me to question God's intentions toward me. They affected the way I owned (or didn't own) my role and responsibility in relationships. And many times, they kept me stuck in patterns that resigned me to a self-image that screamed "second best." Much like my eye doctor prescribes contact lenses to correct my nearsightedness, I would come to see that my Eve vision needed an adjustment to the truth. But at least I wasn't alone.

A closer study, and even a stroll through Eve's lengthy Wikipedia page, revealed a troublesome reality: throughout Christian history, Eve was often seen as a temptress. A sexual temptress. This led many church fathers to express the view that women couldn't be trusted, that they were danger waiting to happen. They were "the devil's gateway," said Tertullian, the man who coined the word "Trinity."[1] Thomas Aquinas claimed that women were inferior to men.[2] And that's just the tip of the iceberg.

More troubling to me than the disparaging comments casting Eve as a bad girl was the complete lack of scriptural support to back them up. We've got Eve issues, all right, but it's not the Bible's fault. Mercifully, God's Word says, "The truth will set you free" (John 8:32). And so I eventually peeled back the pages of Scripture to uncover the truth about the real Eve of Eden.

Along the way, I realized that for many if not most of us, it is Eve's sin that defines her. Those irrevocable moments when she sought wisdom apart from God. If only she hadn't listened to the serpent. If only she hadn't pursued her own self-importance. If only she hadn't eaten the fruit. If only Adam had stopped her. If only.

Here's the difficult truth: Eve's disobedience colors the way we feel about ourselves as women, even when we don't admit it. I'll say it again another way. The way you feel about Eve reflects the way you feel about yourself. If Eve is dangerous, you are dangerous. If Eve is gullible, you may be gullible too. If Eve is inferior, then surely something about women in general is simply not up to par.

So, tell me, what's a girl to do with the problem of Eve?

UNFREEZING EVE

Rendezvousing with the serpent. Believing the lie. Biting the fruit. In the story of Eve, many of us have pressed the pause button, flash-freezing Eve as she grabs a shiny apple or sinks her teeth into a luscious piece of fruit. But what if the primary truth about Eve is different from our strongest impressions of her? What if the most memorable images in our Bible story books neglected to communicate Eve's true identity? And what if we've skipped over a portion of her story that holds the keys to our own identity as God's daughters?

Only God's Word can unlock the answers. And unlock them it does, if only we look close enough. When we do, we discover God's glorious vision for women created in his own image, as strong agents of rescue in his kingdom, and the ideal finishing touch to his very good creation. (Yes, keep reading—there's more good news!)

We understand that both Adam and Eve sinned in the garden, that they broke relationship with God—and that sin now colors our human experience, making this world a battleground for the heart of every man and woman. Tragically, we know we are born into sin. But we also understand that as daughters of Eve we can now embrace a new reality: the power of Christ's victory over evil. What the serpent cleverly disguised as power and wisdom has been revealed as fallen. What Satan came to steal, kill, and destroy, Christ came to redeem and restore. "Therefore, if anyone is in Christ, *the new creation* has come: The old has gone, the new is here!" (2 Corinthians 5:17, emphasis added).

And so we press the play button, unfreezing Grandmother Eve. Yes, the beauty of Adam and Eve's partnership devolved into a selfish battle for individual power. But the story must not end there; indeed, it doesn't end there. Hold on tight, for our story, as described by author Scot McKnight, takes a dramatic turn: "The good news story of the Bible is that the fall eventually gives way to new creation; the fallen can be reborn and recreated . . . The implications of the fall are being undone for those who are in Christ."[3]

As we unfreeze Eve, we set ourselves free to discover her anew in the Bible's first pages. And in doing so, we will discover ourselves—or perhaps recover ourselves—as women created with astounding intention and purpose. For as we awaken Eve from the pages of the Genesis creation story, we begin to understand her vital importance to God's cause.

What we learn next will take us beneath the layers of any girl's or woman's exterior to the biblical truth regarding her soul-DNA. It will most likely excite us, move us, and stretch us. And the journey will start at the beginning, in Genesis 1.

"IN THE BEGINNING . . .

. . . God created the heavens and the earth" (Genesis 1:1).

"All he had to do was speak and there was light," the teacher would say. Clothed in what was most likely a pastel polyester dress, I eagerly soaked in the wisdom of my early Sunday school teacher. I could see God stretching out his hand, and with a poof and perhaps some smoke, light appearing. I innocently pictured the same method being used to make elephants, insects, plants, and great bodies of water. In my little mind, creation was a cosmic magic show, and God the Father, the ultimate show-stopping magician. The great illusionist David Copperfield had nothing on the Creator of the universe.

No one I know remains truly neutral about the Genesis creation account. God's creative power demands a response, an acceptance or rejection, and so thousands of books have been written about whether God did this, and how he did this, and even why he did this. Since the first book of the Bible isn't a science textbook, we can't completely answer all of those questions. (Though that hasn't stopped many from trying.) But every Jesus follower I know does seem to agree on this: the creation account attempts to tell us who we are, if only we will listen. I personally think Genesis 1–3 should come with its own warning label. *Handle with care: clues to your identity contained here.*

At age five, it was God's magic show of creation that enthralled me. At age forty, it is the universal beauty and truth contained in the first chapters of Genesis. Open your Bible to its very first chapter and you'll discover it for yourself: Genesis 1 speaks clearly to people of every age, at any time, in every situation, in any location on this great planet. It's not hard to understand that God existed before the earth did, that he created the earth and the heavens and everything in them, and that he did all of this with incredible intention and purpose.[4] We find comfort in knowing God creatively brought into existence the light and the darkness, the plants and the animals, the oceans and the dry lands.

We understand that the earth we stand on and the heavens we gaze at didn't happen by happy accident: God created them. We recognize God's power in this and take comfort in his loving creativity and provision. And the wonder of it all is that he created this sustainable planet with people in mind. With Adam and Eve in mind. To get a bit more personal, with *you* in mind.

So far so good, right? That depends. If you want to stick with the cosmic creation magic show of your youth and go no further, you might be tempted to disengage. If you've got Eve issues of your own, you might prefer to leave the first couple frozen in the freeze-frame of their sin. At least nothing would change, and you could resume life as you know it. I'm hoping, though, that you'll choose what's behind door number three. For woven into God's intentions for his first humans remains a plan that can literally change the world. Where loneliness reigns, God yearns for community. Where hatred flourishes, God longs for respect and love. And where injustice bubbles up, God aches for equality and impartiality.

Truth be told, "God has never given up on his original dream."[5] A man and a woman placed in a garden, created to love him, to partner with each other, and to creatively and peacefully rule over the earth he created together. Do you long for what God longs for? Does your heart rise up to agree with God's original dream? No wonder: for this is your story, daughter of Eve. The story you were made for.

LET'S GET THIS PARTY STARTED

"Mom, are Jesus and God married?" asked three-year-old Andrew. You've got to chuckle when a preschooler attempts to unravel the marvelous mystery of the Trinity! Right from the beginning, the creation story affirms the presence of a three-in-one God—God the Father, the Son, and the Holy Spirit. The Spirit or *Ruach* makes its appearance in Genesis 1:2, and John the apostle reminds us that in the beginning was the Word, Jesus Christ, who was active in all of creation. This is the creator God: a God of relationship longing for even more community. And those he creates would be beautifully interdependent together, just like their Creator.

I have yet to meet anyone who doesn't want to know where he or she came from, who doesn't want to know he or she was ushered into the world in love. It explains why I rehearse to my niece Cassie the holy moment I witnessed her coming into the world, as I stood nearby with tears of joy on my face. Whether biological children or adopted children, boys and girls want to be assured that there was a great story being told by their entrance into the world—a grand reason for celebration.

I believe that's why the creation story in Genesis speaks so profoundly to us. The garden of Eden, created by God's own hand, flourished and teemed with plant and animal life, and God himself called it "good" (Genesis 1:1-25). But it wasn't until Adam and Eve were fashioned that God announced things were "very good."

That defining moment marks the time when God the Creator's grand vision for men and women fully expressed itself. Adam, Eve, and God started relating to, enjoying, and appreciating one another. The celebration of community commenced! The party, indeed, had started.

The party God started in the garden of Eden brings a smile to my face, until I realize how far we've flown from his original idea. History shows us that God's plan for men and women working together has so often gone terribly wrong. Perhaps you and your husband have entered into World War III in your kitchen, or you've endured abuse from a man who should have been protecting you. Maybe you've noticed the sheer number of women around the world who daily face injustice and outright brutality. Even the privileged American woman who has the right to vote and the opportunity to pursue employment almost anywhere still struggles to come together with her brothers in whole, joyful relationship. And in the middle of the mess, I believe the heart of God weeps.

At times I wonder if we as followers of Jesus are truly pursuing our Creator's dream for us in the place it matters most: in the kingdom of God. "I would have given her [the church] my head, my hand, my heart," wrote nurse Florence Nightingale in the 1800s. "She would not have them. She did not know what to do with them. She told me to go back and do crochet in my mother's drawing room."[6]

Sadly, Ms. Nightingale might have written those words last week. Did God really mean for women to be full, card-carrying members in his kingdom—or did he relegate them to second best?

Did our Creator create us to look beautiful while our brothers bear the bigger load for advancing his cause? Or did he mean what he said when he put two image-bearers in a garden and asked them to rule together over his very good creation?

EVE AS GOD'S IMAGE-BEARER

First, let's look at the humans God created from the way he primarily identified them, the way he *knew* them. After all was said and created, save humankind, God made a stunning announcement in Genesis 1:26-27:

> Then God said, "Let us make mankind in our image, in our likeness, so that they may rule over the fish in the sea and the birds in the sky, over the livestock and all the wild animals, and over all the creatures that move along the ground." So God created mankind *in his own image, in the image of God* he created them; male and female he created them. (Emphasis added)

God, in community with himself within the Trinity—God the Father, the Son, and the Holy Spirit—held a meeting. "Let *us* make mankind in our image, in our likeness . . ." What an outrageous proposal! What he proposed, what pleased him, was to make humans resemble him. Are you so familiar with this passage that you've forgotten how shocking this is? God made you, as a woman, to be like him!

Suppose you had lived in the time when Genesis was written and witnessed this outlandish idea. Let's say you were listening as the scroll containing the creation account was read aloud in the Hebrew language. I imagine this might be your response: *Come again?!*

For in the ancient Near East culture there was one thing generally understood: only kings who ruled were made in the image of deity. This, in fact, gave them the right to rule. So right here, in

Genesis 1, God himself is making clear that the humans he creates "share the status of royalty."[7]

What could this mean, daughter of Eve, except that you resemble God? And that you represent him in this world. Let's keep reading in the first chapter of Genesis:

> God blessed them and said to them, "Be fruitful and increase in number; fill the earth and subdue it. Rule over the fish in the sea and the birds in the sky and over every living creature that moves on the ground." (Genesis 1:28)

God's instruction to have children is not a command, but a blessing. So we know we have not fallen short if we do not physically have a child. But for both man and woman, this short paragraph contains definite marching orders. *Male and female, go out filling the earth, ruling it, and taking care of it.*

Note that you as a female are not given a role, but a responsibility, together with Adam. You (and every male and female in this world) are given broad, sweeping instructions to represent God by using and caring for and creatively overseeing his good world. The Creator of the world has some high expectations for you, and he delights in seeing each of his children fulfill them.

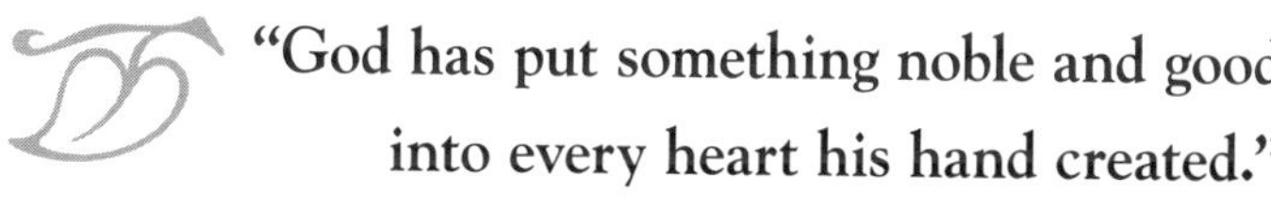

"God has put something noble and good into every heart his hand created."

—Mark Twain

God's intentions toward us are both humbling and awe-inspiring. We are made in the *imago Dei*—or image and likeness of God—and so something about us reveals something about our Creator. In the Old Testament, the word *image* stood for forms and shapes of idols, while the word *likeness* describes a similarity. We are formed to be similar to God, not physically but in our personality or nature and in our ability to make moral decisions. So while Adam and Eve looked at each other, taking in the image of God in one another, they were simultaneously commissioned for serious business: to be God's representatives in the world.[8]

If God wanted someone stronger for the job, he might have commissioned a lion or a bear. But God wanted beings who were similar to him, a man and a woman who could rule by the "power of their minds and personalities."[9]

He could have chosen two creatures who would have been equal in their physical strength. But God made a strong statement by creating a man *and* a woman. Though the man was physically stronger, the woman displayed a facet of God's image that only she could reflect. And so Adam and Eve stood equal before God, complementing one another, offering their uniqueness to cooperate and collaborate as partners.

Making Eve in God's own image not only says something strong and wonderful about every woman in the world but also says something fascinating about her Creator. He can be recognized in the strong characteristics of both male and female image-bearers, because he transcends the categories we understand.

He is sovereign over all and incomprehensible, and we as image-bearers are left in wonder. For as we go about our homekeeping, our careers, our childrearing, and our ministries, we are interacting directly with other image-bearers—beautiful beings made in the very likeness of God. Astounding.

We are created to be the very likeness of God to this world. And because of his good plans for us, and his work in us, we are also created to represent him. This is true for each of us whether or not we recognize God as Creator and Sustainer. The question Eve had to answer and every woman after her is this: *Do I represent God well?*

Perhaps we've now pressed play, unfreezing Eve from the story of her sin and setting us free to discover God's plan for Eve and every woman after her. I imagine "storybook Eve" transforming into the woman who clearly displays God's grand intentions for his daughters. We as women are fully made in the image of the almighty God. He cared so much about our sin problem that he made a gracious plan of rescue through his Son. He promises to restore our hope and redeem our hearts, if we trust in him.

And yet.

There's still a nagging uncertainty, buried beneath Sunday morning smiles and well-intentioned hearts. If all this good news is true, then why did God create woman after man? Is Eve's primary vocation in life to serve Adam? Did the Creator of all say anything else about his intentions for Eve and every woman after her?

As a matter in fact, he did. I personally believe he made a statement twice in Genesis 2 that might just amaze you. It's buried beneath centuries of biblical study that quickly dismissed Eve as Adam's "helper." Admittedly, scholars say it's not easy to translate Hebrew into English. But along the way, throughout our Christian history, Eve has often been painted as an inferior helper to Adam. Let's just say that something vitally important has been lost in translation.

For if she is a helper, Eve is a helper as God himself is a helper to his people. Read the last sentence again to make sure you got it right. For plain as day in Genesis 2, verses 18 and 20, God uses the Hebrew word *ezer* (seen as "helper") to describe Eve. It just so happens this same word is used sixteen times in the Old Testament to describe God himself and how he comes through for his people in a time of great difficulty.[10]

Without further adieu, let me present . . .

EVE AS *EZER*

The Lord *God said, "It is not good for the man to be alone. I will make a helper* [ezer] *suitable for him"* (Genesis 2:18).

Hot tears splashed down my cheeks as my new husband stared at me in confusion. I had been studying the creation story when I stumbled across the strong Hebrew word God used when creating Eve: the *ezer.* In that moment, God's intentions leapt off of the printed page and started a revolution in my heart. I never would have guessed how highly God thinks of his daughters. I hadn't understood how invaluable we are to his kingdom. I felt a strange combination of exhilaration and anxiety about what it would mean to stand shoulder to shoulder with my Christian brothers, instead of taking my usual safer back row seat.

The tears eventually dried, but the question remained: Would I be willing to follow the blueprint I discovered in God's Word, or would I shrink back in fear? The journey for me would mean reevaluating why I wasn't using some of my spiritual gifts, asking what God meant for my marriage relationship, and reimagining how I and my sister-*ezers* could more effectively join with our brothers in Christ to better serve a world that desperately needs God's love.

A few years have passed since my initial discovery, but since then I've become even more convinced of the necessity of women fulfilling the original purpose God called them to in the garden of Eden. So let's rejoin the place where it all began—the unfolding creation story in Genesis 2. Unlike Genesis 1, God zooms in to give us a more detailed account of the creation of Adam and Eve.

Picture this: Adam lovingly placed in a garden of exquisite beauty; surrounded by animal couples of every form, color, and kind; with plenty of food and drink, and a benevolent Creator to enjoy. But following the animal parade, in which Adam named the creatures God had created, we get the first hint that things are not as they should be, that God himself isn't satisfied.

Although up until this point God had declared all things "good," he now makes a startling statement in Genesis 2:18: "It is *not* good . . ." That is, "It is *not good* for the man to be alone. I will make a helper [*ezer*] suitable for him" (emphasis added).

Let's see. It is not good for man to be alone, so I will make him a servant or a slave. Nope. It is not good for man to be alone, so I'll create someone who will be a slight help to him in the future. Not hardly. "It is not good for the man to be alone, so I will make [an *ezer*] suitable for him." An agent of rescue suitable for him!

Let me be clear:

> God could have used a Hebrew word meaning "female slave," but he didn't.
>
> He might have used any of the Hebrew words meaning "wife," but he chose not to.
>
> God offered a strong word used repeatedly in the Bible to describe how he comes through for his people in a time of desperate need.[11]

There are only two options in translating the word *ezer* into English. Either the woman is a "strong helper" as God is a strong helper, or she is a "strong power." The full force of the original meaning of this verse might come out something like this: *to end the loneliness of the single human, I will make another strong power, corresponding to it, facing it, equal to it. And the humans will be both male and female.*[12]

Put that on your next job application or medical form under occupation: *I'm a strong power.* For not only has God identified you as his image-bearer, but he also chose back in the garden of Eden to identify you as a strong power. Nowhere in these two primary keys that unlock your identity do we find a hint of female inferiority or a whiff of male superiority. Instead, we find the beauty of an interdependent relationship formed by a God of relationship.

Let that sink in for a moment. One woman I know so embraced her newfound identity as a strong power that it changed her perspective on life's challenges. While experiencing a no-good, very-bad day, she stopped in the middle of the supermarket and began singing: "I am an *ezer*, and I can do all things through Christ who gives me strength." And a female college student who heard the *ezer* message raised her hand to say that she had not planned to vote in an election, but the *ezer* message had changed her mind.

As the "strong power" was created from Adam's side, it became clear that Eve was not another animal, but was a perfect ally and companion. The creation account will soon draw to a close, but before it does, we witness the forming of Eve as God's ideal finishing touch.

WHAT THE *EZER* ISN'T

After my initial tears and excitement over my discovery of the *ezer*, I began to wonder what it all meant. What made an *ezer* . . . an *ezer*? For just as this one word ties women everywhere together, our stark differences also remain. Only an imaginative God would create a woman such as Mother Teresa, who spent her heart and life on India's poor. He alone was the One who also created the Michele Bachmanns and the Hillary Clintons of the world, the homemakers extraordinaire, female secretaries and business executives, and the many women who serve as prominent and not-so-prominent church leaders. In this dizzying display of diversity, what exactly does it mean to be an *ezer*?

Here in the creation story, in the primary passages God uses to define and describe who men and women are, we find something totally, noticeably missing: a detailed description of gender roles. Yes, it becomes clear that the woman will carry and give birth to children (Genesis 3:20), but any other ideas we get about individual duties or responsibilities are absent. That leaves us with a wide range of possibilities for a specific calling on any one woman's life. Rather than limiting us, being an *ezer* (strong helper) sets us free!

Even the short, but significant list of things a strong helper is not unleashes each woman to her full potential in whatever situation she finds herself.[13] Let's review them:

A domestic servant. Think of it! Adam hardly needed a cook, since they picked the perfect nutrition required off the plants in the garden. There was no cleanup, since they lived in the great outdoors. And as far as clothes, who needs 'em? The Bible says they were "naked, and they felt no shame" (Genesis 2:25). Adam didn't need a servant at all, but a strong partner.

You know as well as I do that women do an amazing amount of homekeeping chores, and that they are often more than capable in this area. It helps me to remember that God has given me the ability to take care of the things he's entrusted to me; he simply hasn't mandated that I must do domestic chores because I'm a woman. It may be part of my weekly responsibilities, but it's not a primary key to my identity.

Defined by marriage or motherhood. Did you notice that Eve was a strong helper before she had sexual relations with Adam? And did you realize that Eve was a complete *ezer*—or strong power—at least nine months before she gave birth to children? This amazing truth, and the fact that God didn't use a word for wife when creating Eve, sets every woman free to be the strong helper and strong power God intended her to be—single or married, mother or not.

If only I had discovered this freeing piece of biblical wisdom in my thirty-five years of singleness! Even now, as I face infertility, I take comfort in knowing I will always be an *ezer*, no matter my social status in life. God has a plan for each of his daughters, and we are defined by his intentions, not by our current circumstances.

Retired. Happily, there is no age limit on being a strong helper. A birth certificate commemorates the entrance of a strong helper into the world, and every woman's funeral reminds us of her on-going legacy. A woman is a strong helper from birth to death, no matter what her circumstance or station in life, and she will be a strong power in God's kingdom until her final breath and beyond.

After hearing a sermon on the *ezer*, one eighty-plus-year-old woman replied, "Thank you. You helped me to realize I am still worth something." Our calling is not determined by our physical strength or our frailty, but by our Creator.

Any other ideas about Eve's secondary status come from the tragedy that unfolded when sin entered the world. As God grieved at the consequences that would come, he made a sad prediction. Adam would rule over Eve. Eve would have pain when bearing children. (Can I hear an amen?) And Adam and Eve would deal with toil and difficulty in their daily work.

These were tough consequences, for sure. But just as Christ came to restore and redeem us (2 Corinthians 5:17), he also came to put our relationships with him and with others right again. God never gave up on his original dream. And neither should we.

RECLAIMING EVE

Remember my friend Ann from the beginning of the chapter? She was partly right. It's not only what happened to Eve in Genesis that wasn't cool but it's also what has happened to her reputation throughout history. But just as we pressed the play button, unfreezing Eve from her sin and examining God's beautiful purposes in creating her, we've begun to reclaim God's original vision for each of his daughters.

My secret grudge against Eve has evolved into a spirit of wonder and hope over all the possibilities that arise when women step into their rightful place in God's kingdom. Imagine what could happen if every woman who follows Christ owned her identity as his image-bearer, resembling and creatively representing God on this earth. Dream with me about the potential of women living out their identity as strong partners with their brothers and sisters in making God's kingdom come on earth as it is in heaven. And consider the possibilities of asking God how you can best use the gifts he's given you to care for the world and the people he's created.

Remember:

> **You are God's image-bearer.** Every female ever born bears God's image, resembling him and representing him in this world.
>
> **You are an *ezer*.** Every woman is a *strong power* created to join with men, advancing God's kingdom, no matter what your station in life.

A woman's biblical identity is broad enough to apply to the mother of five who homeschools her children, to the fifteen-year-old worshipping the Lord in the church praise band, the professional working woman, the full-time single missionary, and any woman who feels limited by her health or social status.

As we close this chapter, let's thank God together that the story of Eve's sin is not the final word. God's plan of rescue through his Son sets us free to recover his original intentions for his daughters. What the real Eve of Eden teaches us is this: *In God's kingdom, every woman—no matter her circumstance—can be reclaimed.*

Questions for Discussion

1. Before reading this chapter, what were your primary impressions of Eve?

2. How does it feel to learn from Scripture that Eve is not inferior to Adam, but that she is God's image-bearer and an *ezer* (a strong power and an agent of rescue)?

3. How does the message that every woman is God's image-bearer and a strong power affect the way you view yourself? How might it affect your future?

Then God said, "Let us make mankind in our image, in our likeness, so that they may rule . . ." (Genesis 1:26)

2 ALLIANCE

WHEN ADAM AND *EZER* UNITE

My boyfriend drove his white Ford pickup down the expressway as he glanced in my direction. We were at a crossroads in our relationship, trying to make a specific decision that would honor God, when I (Suzanne) smiled and said, "Well, I'm glad I don't have to worry about it. It's your responsibility." His head quickly whipped around as he exclaimed, "This is a democracy—not a dictatorship!"

For the moment, I sat motionless, stunned. Didn't the Bible say men are in charge and women need to submit? Did my boyfriend, J., have the self-contained strength and wisdom to know how to make this decision? Did he truly need my help, or did he just want it? In a few short seconds, I wondered what his statement said about us, and maybe more importantly, what it said about me.

"OK," I said, cautiously glancing his direction. "Well, I think . . ." The decision J. and I came to that day protected our relationship, kept our eyes focused on God's plan for us, and greatly minimized our regrets, even when our relationship eventually dissolved. It was a choice informed by both our viewpoints, surrounded by each of our experiences, and decided on as the Holy Spirit moved in each of our hearts. It was a solid decision, made possible by the weight of an alliance intended by God.

The *adam* and the *ezer* were shoulder to shoulder, side by side. "It is not good for the man to be alone," said God in Genesis 2:18. "I will make a helper [*ezer—strong power corresponding to him*] suitable for him." My twenty-six-year-old self had never thought much about the role I might play someday in a marriage relationship, except for the imagined relief I would feel at having someone else make decisions for me. That day J. made me reevaluate my desire to disengage with men in general and instructed me on just how valuable a man-woman alliance can be in getting the job done.

And no wonder: this was God's idea from the very beginning. Years would pass before I would truly grasp the beauty of the *adam* and the *ezer* partnering together to accomplish much more than either could separately. God's proclamation that all was "very good" didn't come until both male and female were created, forming an alliance that would take dominion over the earth by filling, caring for it, and creatively ruling over it.

I happily admit it now—J. was right all along: no one benefits when a woman sits on the sidelines, unwilling or unable to contribute fully. The combination of the *ezer* and the *adam* was intrinsically built to further God's cause. So when women don't show up—when they can't or won't show up—everyone loses.

This is true when a boyfriend and a girlfriend make decisions about their relationship. It can be observed every day as men and women do, or don't, interact in businesses around the world. You might have noticed it at your son's or daughter's soccer game or in a project to serve the poor. This principle lies at the heart of our marriages and in the church Jesus himself came to build.

The promise is this: when God's image-bearers come together, male and female, unselfishly offering their uniqueness and their gifts to get a job or a ministry or a relationship started, something undeniable happens. We are all better for it. God smiles in delight as his kingdom marches forward. Just the act of partnering together reflects the glory and beauty of our Creator through the irreplaceable team he built. We've all observed what happens when men and women do this poorly, as can be seen in homes and brothels, in workplaces and churches around the globe. But, ah, when we do it well! When I see male and female image-bearers partnering with joy, it makes me believe again. It makes me believe this blessed alliance God created and intended truly can change the world.

A PARTY OF TWO

I'll never forget the day when I (Carla) made one of my first trips to St. Louis to visit with my future husband Chuck's parents. They were wonderful people, serving God together in ministry, although in very traditional roles. Dad Sunberg was the pastor, while Mom Sunberg was the wife and homemaker. The meals served in that home were some of the tastiest on the planet and usually ended with some kind of homemade pie. For Chuck specifically, there was always a coconut custard pie, which had been prepared with great love for their oldest son.

On this one occasion, however, it was what happened later that afternoon that caught my attention. In hindsight, I'm not sure that I ever saw Dad Sunberg do anything domestic. That particular Sunday afternoon he was sitting in his favorite recliner as the entire world seemed to hustle and bustle around him. Mom had been working in the kitchen making dinner, and now cleaning up. Other family members were helping with the kitchen work when I heard a rattling coming from the direction of the recliner. I looked over and there was Dad with a large tumbler of what had been iced tea. All that remained was ice, and he was shaking his cup so that Dolly (as he affectionately called Mom Sunberg) would notice. He wanted more. Though he never said a word, he continued to rattle his ice. In that moment, Mom stopped what she was doing and ran off to fill his cup. Chuck says he remembers the look I shot his direction. Honestly, I think I was shocked because I'd never quite witnessed something like that, and I think my expression probably communicated what I was feeling inside: "Don't even try that."

❧❧❧

In our early years of marriage we realized both of us had brought preconceived notions of our roles to the relationship, many of which were formed from our parents. As we began to learn what it meant to be a *blessed alliance*,[1] we discovered a way of partnering to help the other. While Chuck was in seminary, I worked full-time as a nurse to help support us financially. At first, my husband couldn't understand why I couldn't also accomplish all the things his mother had done around the house while he reclined in the living room. Then one day he said to me, "I don't know how to cook, but I know how to do dishes. How about when we come home you do the cooking, and I'll rest a little, and then after supper, I'll clean up so you can rest." That was the first of many things that he has done to allow me to flourish and to be a full partner in the *blessed alliance*.

Today we even share a job, as co-superintendents, giving oversight to over seventy churches. We are equal partners in all that we do, whether at home, with family, or on the job. Looking back, I know that Chuck's parents deeply loved one another, and Mom served Dad out of the love and respect she had for him. At the same time, I'm not sure that either one of them ever felt they could spread their wings and be set free from the roles that had been thrust on them. In their minds, they simply accepted these boundaries for their lives.

Over the years, I've come to believe God intended something more with the creation of Adam and Eve. Men and women were to work together as equals, each bringing their skills and abilities to the tasks before them. The resultant synergy made them more effective as a team than they could ever be as separate individuals. There is beauty and power in this party of two!

One of the greatest husband-wife alliances in recent history can be seen in William and Catherine Booth, founders of the Salvation Army. Both William and Catherine had to wrestle with what it meant to be a team, and for each to be a part of this *blessed alliance*. They were both very gifted individuals who accepted one another as equals and partners. They each preached the Word and developed numerous ministries based on their gifts, taking their cue from what the Bible says about each person offering their gifts. Together, they realized that spiritual gifts are not based on gender differentiation but are poured out among God's faithful, male and female alike. That's why the Booths became a powerhouse of influential change, serving God among the needy individuals of England. The result? The birth of the Salvation Army, which has continued to minister to our world for nearly 150 years. Maybe the next time we go by one of those red buckets at Christmas we can remember that it was a *blessed alliance* that energized a couple to follow God's vision for touching the world. What a party!

IT'S ALL ABOUT RELATIONSHIPS

This type of relationship was God's original plan for humankind, and the word *relationship* is the key. God, in the Holy Trinity, reveals to us the design for a holy relationship of love in which there is mutual submission among all the parties. It is in this relationship where we discover the Father who loves the Son, and the Son who loves the Father, who loves the Spirit. It continues with the Father who loves the Son, who loves the Spirit, who loves the Father, who loves . . . well, you get what I mean. Within this relationship there is an intermingling of the hearts of the Father, the Son, and the Holy Spirit that some have referred to has a "holy dance."[2]

It is an intermingling not only of hearts but also of desires and passions. The Son knows the heart of the Father, and the Spirit moves in direct response to the motivations of the Father. That's why Jesus can submit to the will of the Father in the garden of Gethsemane—the Father's will is *his* will. The things that break the Father's heart break Jesus' heart, and the Spirit joins in the response. Within the triune God we find a community of holy love, and it is this relationship that is meant to be reflected in all of humanity. We become God's image-bearers to relationships that are found in community. That's why Jesus can sum up the Law with loving God and loving neighbor.

In Eve, God had created a neighbor for the *adam*. Once she was created, the need for relationship within humanity was met, and the very same image that existed in the Trinity could now be revealed in humankind. This is why Eve became the crowning achievement of all of creation! Humanity now revealed the same love that was found in God.

Sadly, most of us only remember the dangerous Eve—the one who sinned. What if we took time to consider what life was like before she and Adam sinned? God described them as being "one flesh," clinging to one another. A deep and passionate love united this couple, resulting in a satisfying physical and emotional relationship on multiple levels. Daily they walked and lived in Paradise as equals and partners in an intimate relationship with one another and their Creator.

A BLESSED ALLIANCE: GREG AND NONNA

Their relationship started out pretty rocky. Greg was not from a Christian home and had some pretty crazy ideas about religion. Nonna sensed the social pressures of the day to be a good wife and to submit to her husband. However, she just knew that she couldn't submit to the point of allowing her husband to go to hell! What in the world was she supposed to do? She decided the best thing to do was to spend time in prayer, seeking God's leading and guidance in her marital relationship. She really loved Greg, but she also knew that he wasn't always making the best decisions in life. Through extended periods of time in prayer and studying God's Word, Nonna began to understand this idea of the *blessed alliance*, and that for her and Greg to truly have the relationship that God wanted, she needed to be his partner, and even, at times, his leader. She would have to take the lead in spiritual matters of the home for him to become everything that God wanted him to be.

It didn't happen overnight, but Greg began to appreciate what he saw in Nonna. After a number of years he gave his life to the Lord and eventually went on to become a minister. Greg Jr. was emotional as he spoke at his father's funeral, reminiscing on the loving relationship he personally witnessed between his mother and father. They had become a powerful partnership, everything that God had intended for Adam and Eve.

Let's open the curtain again on the situation in Paradise. Sadly the party in the garden comes to a screeching halt and the idyllic picture is lost. On a daily basis Adam and Eve had enjoyed a leisurely stroll through the garden fellowshipping with one another and with God. On one of those days as they walked together they were confronted by the Serpent. With his cunning words he encouraged them to defy God and to eat of the forbidden fruit. Eve stepped forward and ate first, and Adam followed. Immediately they knew that something was wrong and a new trajectory was plotted in which relationships began to crumble. The couple that had been so comfortable with one another as "one flesh" were suddenly embarrassed at their nakedness. As they sought out clothing, the fig leaves became a barrier between the two of them, foreshadowing what was to come. What we have always accepted as a punishment—"your desire will be for your husband, and he will rule over you" (Genesis 3:16)—was not a new commandment from God, but rather a prophetic statement regarding the change in the relationship between Adam and Eve.

WHAT ABOUT SUBMISSION?

Not long ago I was at a wedding where the minister made it a point to look directly at the bride and to admonish her to always submit to her husband. However, that's as far as it went. There was no encouragement for the husband to love his bride, just as "Christ loved the church and gave himself up for her" (Ephesians 5:25). Something is wrong with this perspective, and sadly it's one that has been perpetuated by the church. For centuries, whether or not intentional, what women have heard is that "men are more valuable to God than women."

Instead of reading the curse as a prophetic word about the results of the fall, we have adopted God's statement as a pronouncement of punishment on women. What happened as a result of the fall was a breakdown in relationships. The man and woman were no longer in a position of equal partnership, but the woman was ruled over by the man. The man no longer had authority over the earth and its creatures, but now had to work and toil the ground. The man and woman were driven out of Paradise, unable to freely walk with God on a casual and personal level. Loving God and loving neighbor became increasingly difficult and by the time the next generation arrived, jealousy between two brothers resulted in the very first murder. Truly when the church, or anyone for that matter, focuses the entire problem of sin and the destruction of relationships on women, we have a problem.

MUTUAL SUBMISSION

The good news is that just as the party came to a screeching halt in Paradise, it began to spring to life again in another garden. In the garden of Gethsemane, Jesus agonized over his Father's plan. For within hours, Jesus would usher in a new era of mutual submission among those united with God. Jesus' impending death on the cross would change everything, providing for the restoration of all relationships: those between God and humankind, and human to human. What is turned upside down in the garden of Eden is turned right side up again in the garden of Gethsemane. It is no wonder that Jesus chooses to have a woman, Mary Magdalene, whose reputation is about as tarnished as Eve's,[3] to be the first one to spread the good news about his resurrection! It is the restoration of Eve, but also of Adam and the original Adam-Eve relationship.

Let's return for a moment to the wedding scene and think about where we sometimes go wrong. I am curious as to why the church has wanted to accept the restoration of humanity's relationship with God but has been hesitant to embrace the restored male-female relationship, instead clinging to the fallen or subordinate position of the woman to the man.

Nearly 150 years ago revival broke out in the northeastern United States. One of the fires that sparked this revival came from the home of a woman, Phoebe Palmer. She invited people to her home at noon on Tuesdays for the "Tuesday meeting for the promotion of holiness." For years people gathered to pray in her home, and numerous women found glorious restoration as God's strong helpers. The women began to embrace this concept of the *blessed alliance* and its accompanying freedom. A well-known Methodist preacher from New York, Rev. Thomas Upham, who had been attending the prayer meetings, wrote, "One of the results of God's great work which is now going on in the world will be to raise and perfect woman's position and character. The darkest page in human history is that of the treatment of woman."[4] Sadly, the church must take some responsibility for that treatment, for she has been resistant to accept the restoration of both of God's image-bearers.

Let's return to the wedding scene, but this time try to put on our Ephesian lenses. Paul clearly believes in the restoration of these relationships and in Galatians 3:28 he says, "There is neither Jew nor Gentile, neither slave nor free, nor is there male and female, for you are all one in Christ Jesus." The letter to the Ephesians is addressed to believers in that city, to whom he is referring in 5:21. Paul states, "Submit to one another out of reverence for Christ." Writing to a church full of new believers, Paul encourages them as followers of Christ to be servants of one another. Within this group of believers then, he speaks to the married couples. They already know how he feels about mutual submission among believers. It is the same type of mutual submission found within the Holy Trinity. Therefore, it has to do with an attitude or posture, one in which we bow down before one another! Having this attitude, wives are reminded that they are to have this type of posture toward their believing husbands. It is a reinforcement of what Paul has already said.

> Husbands, love your wives, just as Christ loved the church and gave himself up for her to make her holy, cleansing her by the washing with water through the word, and to present her to himself as a radiant church, without stain or wrinkle or any other blemish, but holy and blameless. In this same way, husbands ought to love their wives as their own bodies. He who loves his wife loves himself. After all, no one ever hated their own body, but they feed and care for their body, just as Christ does the church—for we are members of his body. "For this reason a man will leave his father and mother and be united to his wife, and the two will become one flesh." This is a profound mystery—but I am talking about Christ and the church. (Ephesians 5:25-32)

ONE FLESH

The profound mystery here is the beautiful relationship that Paul had envisioned for a husband and wife. It is the restoration of the "one flesh." This relationship is one that seeks to help the other become everything that God would want him or her to be. It includes a wife looking after her husband and helping him to develop beyond his dreams. It is a husband allowing his wife to utilize all the talents and abilities bestowed upon her to develop into the holy woman of God she was created to be.

The two are called to work together as one, each bringing his or her diverse gifts and abilities to the party. Everyone loses out when the diverse talents that God has created are not put to use within a marital relationship. Remember the parable of the talents? Why would God give a woman a boatload of talents and then just expect her to bury them in the backyard? That's not the kind of God we serve. Instead, he expects men and women, husbands and wives to bring all their talents, uniting them together and watching the exponential energy that results from their union. That is what God intended!

Bill Hybels is well known as the senior pastor of the Willow Creek Church near Chicago, Illinois. As a young man he was busy growing his church and his ministry and he accepted what he had been told by the church about husband-wife relationships. The result was that his wife was unfulfilled as she tried to fit into that subordinate role. As a result she became depressed, and the two of them sought out what the Scriptures really had to say about women and their place within relationships. Since that time she has become an equal partner together with her husband. Bill and Lynne Hybels have developed a *blessed alliance*. He speaks glowingly of her ministry around the world, as he often keeps the home fires burning in Chicago:

> Through Lynne, I've had the opportunity to learn two important lessons. First, that women who are freed, challenged, and empowered to develop their gifts and pursue the passion planted in them by God do not become less loving wives or less devoted parents. On the contrary, they bring a greater level of joy and energy to every dimension of life. I can honestly say that now, during Lynne's most intense and authentic ministry involvement, she is also offering her very best self as a wife, mother, grandmother, daughter, and friend. I only regret that I did not help her discover this way of life years ago.[5]

When husbands and wives become servants of one another, the result is a union that is beyond our comprehension, one that Paul referred to as a "profound mystery." Instead of one appearing as the weaker partner and the other as the stronger, they become a strong tower together, united in their love for God and love for one another. The opinions of each are necessary and valued if the union is to grow and develop. Each person in the relationship becomes more of a person than they ever thought possible, because each works to bring out the best in the other. It is the profound mystery of Christ and the church—Jesus Christ, who loves his bride, the church, so much that he is willing to do anything to make her beautiful and to save her. The church, his bride, praising and worshipping him for all that he has done for her, to make her what she is!

Recently my husband and I were traveling to a rather difficult church meeting. We knew that there was the possibility that things would not go smoothly. Along the way we began to have a conversation about the *blessed alliance*. We realized that we had begun to take this alliance for granted as it had become normal for us. Had either one of us been going to that meeting alone we would have had to take someone else with us. Since we were a *blessed alliance* we were able to go to the meeting together, and the synergy created by the two of us allowed us to work through the difficulties as a team. Surprisingly, the evening ended in a beautiful time of prayer with the members present. We weren't sure that would have happened had only half of the alliance been present. This is God's plan, for sons and daughters to unite, helping each to be significantly stronger than they ever would be alone.

SIBLINGS IN CHRIST, UNITE

A funny thing happens when you start writing about Christian sisters and brothers becoming allies. You start to analyze (and sometimes overanalyze) your male-female relationships in the past and present. You wonder how it all works, exactly. How do a man and woman form a strong team? What makes sisters and brothers click—and what makes them clash? Cutting through the questions, Shari's direct message popped up on my (Suzanne's) Facebook screen. Though she was halfway around the world, I could picture her typing with a smile on her face, her heart bubbling up and spilling out onto her keyboard.

Earlier in the day, I had posted a question on Facebook, asking friends to submit stories of men and women working together for the good of his kingdom. Responses trickled in, including the mention of a husband and wife co-pastoring a church, of male and female nurses working side by side in the hospital, of marketing professionals using their creativity and skill and partnership to promote worthy causes.

I enjoyed all of the responses, but Shari's private message grabbed me. As a single female missionary in a war-torn Muslim country, Shari was often alone—literally and figuratively. I knew from our previous conversations that she was in danger on a regular basis, and that—if need be—she was prepared to give her life for the cause of the gospel. One of the amazing stories she shared when she visited the States was that she had once been out walking when a man in a trench coat approached her. When he opened up his coat to flash her, Shari struck back, punching him in the face. Talk about being a strong power and an agent of rescue!

Here is more of Shari's story in her own words:

> As a single woman in a context where men and women do not interact as freely as in America, I don't have many substantive conversations with men, and my heart longs for that, for brothers to speak into my life, for protection. One time at team meeting, I was being arrogant and rebellious and "doing my job" but not loving team members or seeking to honor them. My team leader, a married guy not much older than me, called me and said, "Hey, can we talk?" Kevin came over, and he actually asked questions. He wanted to know what I was thinking, where I was coming from, and he gently led me to see the priority of the team over my individual busyness. I felt so honored and cared for that this guy would be willing to deal with me and seek to develop trust and make the effort to show me he cared about me as a sister and colleague.
>
> I suppose it's also no surprise that I often feel exposed and vulnerable and afraid. I am sufficiently arrogant enough to attempt to travel alone to remote villages. However, there have been times when the men on my team make efforts to come alongside me or even offer to speak on my behalf. I am accustomed to doing a lot on my own, but when these brothers initiate and want to serve and protect me, their sister, it is powerful. And it starts to melt my fearful, guarded heart.

Shari's message made me stop and consider how desperately she needs her brothers. I picture her walking down a dusty, broken road, with a Bible hidden underneath the burka she wears for her own protection. She is ready to take the gospel to whomever God places in her path. And then I picture her walking down the same road with a brother or two by her side. I picture these men offering up their physical, emotional, and spiritual strength on her behalf. Not because they are married to her, or because she is their biological sibling or their mother, but because she is their spiritual sibling. Because Shari has been called to carry the gospel through word and deed to a place that scares most of the rest of us to pieces. And because, as her brothers, these men feel uniquely responsible to partner with her and to protect her.

Sometimes I wonder if our brothers understand how desperately we long to and need to partner with them: how much we need them in our corner. Other times, I wonder if we as women realize how indispensable we are to the team God built in the beginning. Consider another story in a very different setting.

Come Sunday morning at 9:15 A.M., a curious thing happens at my church. Jamie, our co-author, walks into her twenty-something ReGeneration Bible class and welcomes them as their teacher. Some of them pop in late, having hit the snooze button one too many times. Occasionally someone even shows up early.

But the curious thing is this: many Sunday mornings Jamie's class is made up entirely of twenty-something men. Except Jamie, of course. It's a new trend, and Jamie and I have been trying to figure out why this might be happening. Oh, and in case you're wondering, Jamie is happily married to our church's youth pastor and the mother of one adorable baby boy. She teaches twice a month, then rotates with a gentleman in our church who teaches the opposite Sundays.

When my curiosity got the best of me, I decided to survey her class by asking them a few questions. Their written answers were short, but telling. These guys appreciated Jamie's class *because* she brought a different perspective than a male teacher would bring, not in spite of it. They believe that Jamie approaches the Bible from a feminine perspective, a perspective that in their words is "different than what most males have." And for some reason they cannot quite put their finger on, they not only want but need her perspective. Perhaps even more compelling is the appreciation the class has for having both a male and a female teacher, each displaying God's image in a distinct, but meaningful way—partnering together to get the job done.

I shared the stories first, because stories have a way of cutting through the emotional clutter that too often shadows our relationships. For too long now, I believe the members of Christ's beautiful body have been walking around making some faulty assumptions about the alliance built to carry out God's mission on earth.

Often I hear statements like these:

"Women complement men."

"No, women are equal to men."

To which I say, *yes*! Must an *ezer* be one or the other? And why, I wonder, would our Creator bother to create two types of humans if there weren't some exciting differences between the two? Something about Eve made her uniquely suitable for Adam, and something about her rescuing him from loneliness tells a beautiful and even mysterious story. Yet if we believe God's intentions in the first chapters of Genesis, we also know that Eve was no shrinking violet, but a strong power sent as an agent of rescue. She was Adam's equal in every way, an answer to something that was lacking.

We don't have to choose between embracing our unique feminine identity and living out our calling as equals alongside our brothers. The gospel tells us an entirely different story:

> Women are not inferior. *Instead, every human being is made in God's image, giving him or her intrinsic and equal value before God* (see Genesis 1:27).
>
> Women are not superior. *There is no favoritism with God* (see Galatians 3:28 and James 2:1).
>
> Women and men were not created to be enemies. *Instead, we are to love one another as Christ loved us* (see John 13:34-35).

And so one alternative remains: Adam and Eve were created to be powerful allies.

Often I feel as though I am standing at a great crossroads in the life of God's church. Since studying God's intentions in the creation story, I have grown even fonder of my brothers in Christ. So much so, that if a brother gives me an opportunity to partner with him for the kingdom, I almost never say no. Yet at times I have become increasingly frustrated at the way women are often shut out from fully participating in the church. A woman named Amy describes the struggle in the book *Resignation of Eve*:

> First of all, it's demeaning to women to tell them they don't qualify for a job simply because they lack a certain body part. Reverse roles for a minute . . . and ask yourself how it would feel if women were in charge and men were disqualified simply because they were unable to give birth . . . More important, as followers of Jesus, when we block, stall, or divert women from using their God-given gifts—including leading—we are being unbiblical.[6]

If you're anything like me, Amy's response took your breath away. I have pored over Scripture, scoured books by theologians, and cried out to God about the gulf between men and women that I see in his church. I read Paul's stern warning about spiritual gifts and the parts of Christ's body each offering their share, and I wonder what is happening when some pieces of that body hear the message "I don't need you!" (see 1 Corinthians 12:21).

When I read through my Bible and I see Deborah leading Barak into battle, Huldah and Miriam prophesying, Tamar single-handedly preserving the lineage of Jesus, Phoebe the deacon carrying the book of Romans to its recipients as a servant of Christ, and Priscilla joining with Aquila to lead a house church, I start to shake my head. I even wonder sometimes if Mary Magdalene would again be rejected as a witness to Christ's resurrection if she showed up today. "I'm sorry, Mary. That's great news and all, but we don't really allow women to serve as evangelists or apostles. I hope you understand."

Still, I am just stubborn enough to believe that what is often a broken alliance can and must function as the *blessed alliance* God intended. I believe the biggest obstacle in the way of our partnership goes back to those first chapters of Genesis, in the place where we discovered the *adam* and the *ezer*. And when we go about the process of reclaiming Eve, we will also find ourselves reclaiming Adam.

TO CURSE OR TO REVERSE THE CURSE? THAT IS THE QUESTION

My friend Natasha spoke through my Skype computer screen as her kinky hair twists began to swing excitedly. "The church is trying to do a little curse modification," she said. Intrigued, I asked her to go on. "Preach it to me, sister," I said, smiling. "I'm listening."

Natasha went back to Genesis 3, where we learn that as a result of sin, Adam will rule over Eve (v. 16). Rather than view this tragedy as a temporary state overruled by Jesus when he ushered in a new kingdom, much of the Christian church has used the curse as a rigid code of conduct for women. A short reading of church history confirms this over and over again.

And, if we're honest, we have to admit that the church as a whole often tells women not just "a wife should submit to her husband's rule" but "a woman should submit to a man's rule, period." This is where things get interesting, as Natasha pointed out. In an effort to modify or downsize the curse, women get confusing messages like these:

> You may not speak out in a church meeting or lead a coed Bible study. But if you would like to become an executive or president of your company or organization, that would be okay with us. I don't see anything wrong with that.
>
> Or,
>
> We don't believe women should preach or teach to men in church. However, we're proud that we've added a female professor to our college faculty to teach male and female students about the Bible.
>
> Or,
>
> When women take leadership roles it destroys society and compromises men's ability to lead well. But just between you and me, if Condoleezza Rice ran for president, I'd vote for her. I'd make an exception.

It is no wonder we, the women in the pews, are often confused at what our place should be in the alliance God created. Have you ever wondered why women in churches are often "allowed" or "not allowed" to do certain things while men are eligible to volunteer for any ministry? Curse modification.

Why do some churches allow a woman to speak behind the pulpit for a "special occasion"? Curse modification.

What about the female missionary who is sent to share the gospel with people in the majority world but who cannot preach or teach when she visits churches in the U.S.? Curse modification.

The results of curse modification can be downright dizzying. When a woman attends a new church, how is she to know if the unwritten rules will be the same? As a result, we as women often live in a world of unspoken limitations and disapproving glances that occur when we step over an invisible line.

At this point, I feel I should confess that I have practiced curse modification myself for most of my life. Haven't you? In a world where men are the majority in power and women are the minority, I tried to accept my role as limited in an effort to uphold Scripture and keep peace in God's kingdom. For that matter, many godly people I know believe that women are to be silent in the church and that it is not biblical for a woman to teach or have authority over a man (see 1 Timothy 2:12 and 1 Corinthians 14:34). I personally am fully convinced these passages must be applied only to specific crises in the early church, but I still love people who believe otherwise. I love that they value God's Word, and I accept them as my brothers and sisters in Christ.

However, I have yet to visit a church where women are truly silenced. I don't believe I've ever entered a church where women are not teaching young men what it means to follow Christ. And I believe there's a reason what we do doesn't match what we say we believe. When we take a closer look at the claims of the gospel, we see that Jesus didn't come to uphold or modify the curse, but to *reverse* it.

"Christ redeemed us from the curse of the law by becoming a curse for us" (Galatians 3:13).

As one author noted, "When we require women to pay over and over again for Eve's transgression with their silence and submission, we negate the full redemptive power of the gospel."[7] Rather than upholding the world's model of sexism and discrimination, through Jesus we are to restore the alliance he intended for human beings in the first place.

We do it for women's sake—for our sisters and our daughters. We do it for men's sake—for our brothers and our sons. But most especially, we do it for the kingdom's sake. For when half of Christ's body takes a seat on the sidelines, withholding their giftedness, the whole body limps. What is at stake is not small, but enormous: it is the ability of the church to bring the healing power of the gospel to a hurting world. For all of these reasons and more, I say, long may the alliance live—and through the power of Christ's death and resurrection, may it be blessed.

THE WAY FORWARD

As a girl, I relished games where the girls played against the boys. When the girls won I would think, *Score one for the team! We really are better than the boys.* When the boys beat us, I would sulk: *let's try that again!* But as an adult, God is transforming me into a woman who seeks out opportunities to team up with my brothers. "Score one for the alliance!" I think, when a brother and I fix a problem, feed the poor, or serve in a ministry. And as I move forward, I pray for grace to continue to follow my Savior's lead.

Instead of raising boxing gloves against the other gender, Jesus encourages us to bend down and wash one another's feet. When the world tells us we'll never be on the same team, our Savior's sacrifice reminds us we are already one in Christ Jesus. Just when we feel discouraged, we hear stories of Shari and Jamie and others who have laid down the boxing gloves and are linking arms with their brothers for the sake of the gospel.

If we are waiting for perfect relationships with our brothers, we will be waiting until Jesus comes again for his bride and all things are made right again. But we don't need perfection: we only need a way forward. In this, our Savior illuminates our path. Rather than encouraging his daughters to limit or silence themselves, he calls them into the limelight alongside their brothers. No records exist of Jesus relegating women to second-class citizenship, but only of raising them up to a higher status than their culture allowed. And just as surely as the gospel sets women free, it sets men free as well: "Love the Lord your God with all your heart and with all your soul and with all your strength and with all your mind," Jesus commands each of us. "And, 'love your neighbor as yourself'" (Luke 10:27). We are not first of all to be known by our ministry opportunities (or lack of them), our differences, or our church affiliation—but by our love.

Earlier in the chapter, you witnessed my former boyfriend's insistence that I take full participation in our relationship. You read about the power of marriages like the Booths, the Hybels, and the Sunbergs in which each partner steps forward, laying everything on the table to form the strongest partnership possible. You took in Shari and Jamie's stories, highlighting the need for us as women to partner with the brothers in our lives. And no doubt, your mind has wandered to the alliance you form with the men in your life—husbands or boyfriends, sons and nephews, uncles, and friends and coworkers. It is our hope that this chapter will push you to dream up even more significant ways to link up with the men and boys in your world—shoulder to shoulder and side by side. A *blessed alliance*, indeed. Created by God, restored by Jesus, and still equipped to change the world.

Questions for Discussion

1. How can partnering together with the *adams* of this world be a reflection of God?

2. What might need to change in a marriage for the *blessed alliance* to be fully realized?

3. What does submission look like in a *blessed alliance*?

4. What are practical ways that *ezers* can partner with *adams* in the workforce or at church?

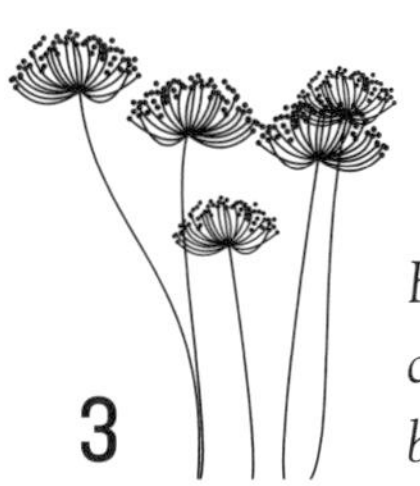

3

But encourage one another daily, as long as it is called "Today," so that none of you may be hardened by sin's deceitfulness. (Hebrews 3:13)

SISTERHOOD

LOVING ONE ANOTHER

I glanced around in nervous anticipation, playing with my car keys. My stomach was tied up in knots. I (Carla) was to meet one of my high school girlfriends for lunch. It had been nearly thirty years since we had seen each other. To be honest, I was worried about all the middle-aged fat I had put on lately. I wondered whether my gray roots would be showing and if I would have the right type of outfit to wear. This girl was so together in high school. She was cute, her hair was always perfect, and she always seemed to be in a good mood with lots of friends. How was I to face her? I was such a nerd in high school. Not your typical nerd, but rather a musical nerd whose only athletic prowess was to be in the marching band. Having been born in Germany, I have never been sure as to whether I've properly understood American culture and language cues. I didn't feel good about myself.

Surprisingly, the conversation over lunch seemed to flow smoothly. It was as if the thirty years had never passed. In the midst of the conversation I mentioned my insecurities from my high school days. I was shocked and amazed to discover that she had similar insecurities. I thought she had it all together. I thought I was the only one who felt the way I did! Women tend to believe, "Other women have it together, but I don't." What I have learned is that most women struggle with their self-image. Sadly, many women and girls do not know what incredible creatures they are, created in the very image of God.

It is time for the negative cycle stemming from a poor self-image to be broken. One way to tackle this is to believe in one another. As women who are reflecting the very image of God, we need to determine that we will become ambassadors for women around us. In 1 Thessalonians 5:11 we are told to "encourage one another and build each other up, just as in fact you are doing." Unfortunately, women, even Christian women, are amazingly skilled at tearing one another down. How often do women at church enter a room for Bible study and then look one another over? "Hmm, Betty's put on a few pounds, hasn't she?" "Sally showed up wearing shorts tonight; if only she could see herself from the backside!" Or, how about the criticism when the lesson is over: "Sandy taught that lesson pretty well tonight, but I think I would have left more time for group discussion."

Whether or not we actually say it out loud, often women are absolutely brutal with one another! Let's take a moment and remember that the other person is a being created in the very image of God. If we thought of one another in this way, maybe we wouldn't be quite so critical.

HOW DO WE SEE ONE ANOTHER?

I am a student of history and love to learn from the stories and lives of those who have gone before us. Whether I'm reading about women from biblical, church, or more modern secular history I am constantly amazed at the common thread that is contained in their stories. It may be the story of Deborah, Ruth, Saint Macrina, Phoebe Palmer, Catherine Booth, Condoleezza Rice, or Jo Anne Lyon, but what emerges is a picture of a woman who allowed God to work on her, to form her in ways that she would never have even imagined. Most of these women were raised in ordinary circumstances, and yet somehow they rose up and for a brief moment they intersected with God in history and touched the world for eternity. Possibly there were a few voices around them that told them they were doing things they should not be doing, that they were not reflecting what it means to be a "good" wife, mother, or woman, but somehow they didn't let those voices get to them. Instead, they responded to the incredible grace of God that reached out to them and drew them into a relationship with Jesus Christ that allowed them to become everything God had intended for them in the very beginning. They became *ezers*, strong and powerful, and a true reflection of a woman created in the image of God.

Unfortunately most of us have inherited a faulty or distorted perception of the image of God in women. At times we have been taught that women were simply an afterthought and, at best, only received half of the image of God. As we've already seen, the result of this kind of teaching is that women have come to believe they are not as valuable to God as men. The Bible tells us God created both male and female in his image, and both men and women have the capacity to reflect God equally. Euclid was a great mathematician who lived in the third century before Christ. He said, "Two things that are equal to the same thing, are equal to each other."[1] God's intent for man and woman was not that they would be identical but that they would be equal partners, equal before God and equal to one another. It was the sin of Adam and Eve that got us into trouble. Humanity was originally created to be a reflection of God to this world, a reflection that would be a perfect representation of Christ. Sadly, sin made us self-centered and we turned inward, so the only reflection that the world could see was of us! The vertical relationship with God has been severely damaged and with it the horizontal relationships as well. This includes our relationships with men and with women. The result is that the sisterhood, which was to empower us, has become a sisterhood that may work to destroy us.

Throughout the years I have learned that the only time I can truly feel secure is when I'm trusting in the Lord. It's when I get my eyes off of Jesus that my insecurities creep out of their hiding place and cause me to doubt myself and God's leading in my life.

When my eyes are off of God and are on me, the result is self-centeredness that fosters my insecurities. Instead of focusing all of my energies on God and on serving him, I worry about myself and this in turn can result in a critical spirit and negativity. It would be nice to believe that I could be immune from this type of response, but sometimes it smacks me in the face when I least expect it!

I had been invited to participate in a conference in Glasgow, Scotland, where we would be celebrating the life of Olive Winchester, a female theologian who was the first woman to graduate with her BD (equivalent to a master of divinity) from the University of Glasgow and then became the first woman to be ordained in any church in the United Kingdom. Celebrating the 100th anniversary of her ordination was a great event that included an academic and ministerial conference as well as a Sunday worship celebration. I had been asked to preach that Sunday morning but was feeling incredibly intimidated by the number of quality female preachers who were present at the event. Before leaving for church, I was in the hotel restaurant eating breakfast and was really struggling with the fact that I was the one who was going to have to preach. A dear friend came over to me and said these kind words, "Remember, it's a sermon, not a competition." Suddenly I sensed that this sister was cheering me on in what I was called to do. I also realized that I was allowing my own personal insecurities to get in the way of what God wanted me to do and that I was not immune to being negative and critical, having a poor self-image.

PAUL'S SOLUTION

Paul had an idea of how we could deal with this negativity. It begins with our focus in life, which must be Jesus Christ. In 2 Corinthians 3:17, Paul tells us, "Now the Lord is the Spirit, and where the Spirit of the Lord is, there is freedom." Christ Jesus is our Lord, and in him we can be set free from the bondage of this world, including the bondage of a poor self-image. When we are filled with the Holy Spirit, the image of God in us is no longer distorted. It is cleaned up and made new. After it is cleaned up and made new, we continue on a journey in which we draw closer to God and in that process the reflection of Christ grows in our hearts and lives until we are transformed into a beautiful and unique likeness of Christ. The result is an image of Christ that reveals all of you that God intended in creation. Interestingly, when we decrease and he increases, we become more of the person God intended for us to be in the first place. John the Baptist reminds us, "He must become greater; I must become less" (John 3:30). This all begins when we give God everything in our lives and allow his Holy Spirit to come into every part of our being, setting us free. This experience is almost like a lightning bolt from heaven that reaches into our personal lives and pours out God's grace through the Holy Spirit into our damaged relationships and helps draw our focus upward, ever gazing into his face.

Paul doesn't stop the lesson there. He goes on to explain that once we experience this blessed grace, the Holy Spirit so fills us that we are set free—set free to continue in a vertical relationship that will be life-altering and life-transforming. Paul tells us that we need to go on and continue the journey of drawing closer to the Lord throughout our entire lives:

> And we all, who with unveiled faces contemplate the Lord's glory, are being transformed into his image with ever-increasing glory, which comes from the Lord, who is the Spirit. (2 Corinthians 3:18)

Every woman with whom you share this journey of faith is being transformed into the likeness of Christ. If we really stopped and thought about the journey on which we all find ourselves, would we be so critical?

BUILDING EACH OTHER UP

That first summer in America was really hard for our whole family (the Sunbergs). Thirteen years earlier we had left the States to live in Russia, and now we had come back to live and to work in Indiana. People kept welcoming us "home" and I know that Christy and Cara, our daughters, and I were just trying to figure out where in the world "home" really was. While Indiana had been home for my husband during his teenage years, I had never lived there before we arrived on that Memorial Day Sunday evening. We had left Moscow early in the morning and traveled with the sun the entire day, and after nearly twenty hours of travel had arrived to our new "home" in Indiana. All I knew is that I felt like a foreigner. I had been born in Germany and had now lived most of my adult life overseas, and suddenly I was to know how to fit in and live in this land that was very foreign for me.

Both Christy and Cara had no recollection of ever having lived in America. Christy would be heading off to college in just a few months and needed to find work for the summer and discovered there wasn't much available for a young girl over the summer break. Finally she got a job as a "sandwich artist" at the local Subway sandwich shop. Even the word "Subway" had all new meaning for us, as it had been the daily mode of transportation for our girls. Christy began to settle into her job, getting to know the people with whom she would work. One of those was Linda, a dear lady in her sixties from the trailer park behind the store who had a sick husband and pregnant daughter at home. Linda certainly did not see herself as an *ezer*—but Christy did! Somehow Christy saw beyond the façade and looked into Linda's heart. She spoke sweetly and gently to Linda every time they worked together. Linda began to respond with a bright smile and an eagerness; she wanted to know what made Christy tick. Christy began to invite Linda to church, but Linda worked most Sundays, and even if she didn't, she had reasons why she couldn't come. Christy, however, didn't give up, and throughout the entire summer she continued to encourage, love, support, and treat Linda with respect. When Christy left for college in the fall there were already noticeable differences in Linda.

I continued to visit Subway long after Christy had left and worked to maintain the relationship with Linda. If they weren't too busy, Linda would come out from behind the counter and give me a big hug and ask me how Christy was doing in college. A few months later, I noticed an attractive new woman sitting on the back row during church. I went to greet her when suddenly she grabbed me and hugged me—it was Linda! She began attending church as much as her work schedule would allow. Another friend at church began to regularly visit Subway as well, just to be an encouragement. We watched as Linda began to grow and literally glow as she was being transformed into the woman that God had created her to be.

When we turn our faces toward Christ and keep our eyes fixed on the Beloved, we become a reflection of the Lord to the entire world. What would happen if we took the words of Paul seriously, and we made a conscious effort to build one another up? What if, instead of allowing our heads to be filled with negative thoughts about one another, to be filled with criticisms, we asked God to fill our minds with praises? And I mean serious, wholehearted praises for one another. Not the half-hearted ones—the type where you shroud your criticism in a compliment. Remember, our negative comments arise from the fact that we don't feel good about ourselves, and self-centeredness creeps in. God's intention is that we build each other up, pulling up one another and pointing others in the direction of Christ. We should help one another to be a reflection of God, being transformed into all the beauty that God had intended in creation.

LOVING THE "DIFFERENT" SISTER

I had just gotten home from a two-week trip to the very frontiers of Central Asia where I had been teaching promising new pastors about church history. My clothing looked rather disheveled, all of which had been worn daily for the entire two-week period in an effort to simply keep warm. What I really craved was a nice hot bath with a chance to soak my frozen body and wash my stringy, greasy hair. As I walked through the door to the apartment, my husband and two beautiful daughters were there to greet me! "Hi, Mommy! We're so glad you're home." "Hey, Mommy, come and see what I made for science class." "Mom, I need to take cookies for school tomorrow, but the kids asked if Dad could make them." Wait a minute—what was that? I stopped short on my way to drop my luggage in the hallway. The kids at school wanted to know if Dad could bake cookies for them?

It had been many years since my husband, Chuck, and I had made that decision to function as an *adam-ezer* team. We were both busy with our assignments on the mission field, he as the field director, and I as the director of theological education. The result was often tag-team parenting where we would take turns being gone for periods of work and training. Along the way we both learned to give and take when it came to traditional roles, and for us, it worked. However, this particular night it stung a little! Making cookies for the kids at school had always been something that I had done. Now, the kids at school liked Chuck's cookies better than mine. It was in that moment that I realized the give and take of being a team and that as we allow God to form us, we may be pushed and pulled and formed into someone we had never imagined. The woman I was becoming was different from the woman I had been early on in our married life. For years as I pursued my education and worked together with my husband, I realized that my life was taking me in a trajectory that might make me "different." And yet, I knew that the trajectory was one that God had created for me and if I were to be obedient, I would need to continue in that direction. For me, to be an *ezer* was to be a student, a teacher, a preacher, a wife, and a mom.

There is a rather persistent concept within Christianity today that a biblical wife will look a particular way. Rachel Held Evans set out on a one-year adventure to see what it might be like to live the life of "biblical womanhood." She struggled with what she had learned in her early years as a young girl growing up in the church. Was there truly just one model for being a Christian woman? She recalled hearing what Dr. James Dobson had taught. "Our ultimate calling, he said, is in the home, where we can serve God and our husbands by keeping things clean, having supper on the table at six, and, most important, making babies."[2] This is not a bad model and for some, this is the right model. The problem is when we encounter another who may be "different." These days there tends to be a bit of a war in the church between what some may view as the more spiritual, "stay-at-home" moms, vs. the "working" moms. And if we are really honest, we would consider the "homeschooling stay-at-home" mom as the ultra-spiritual mom. But some of you may find yourselves in my shoes, wondering if it's okay to be "different."

It was the Lord who challenged me to be obedient to the calling that would take me in a direction in which I might appear to be "different." It was through my personal experience that I began to understand God's unique call for each one of his strong helpers. No two women are alike because God's creativity made each of us to be one of a kind. That's why there's no place for "mommy wars" within the sisterhood! These days God is calling all women; married, single, moms, single moms, working-outside-the-home moms, and stay-at-home moms to present a united front as God's crowning touch of creation. If each woman is a jewel of God's creation, the combination fills the Father's crown with stunning gems producing a symbol of regal authority more beautiful than anything we could ever imagine. There is no "different" in God's design, only special and unique!

THE "CALLED" ONES

"They just don't like me!" she cried into the phone. It was yet another female pastor who had just completed an interview at a church where the major opposition to her potential leadership came from the women on the church board. While no one seemed able to pinpoint why they didn't want her to be the pastor, there continued to be unexplainable opposition. It seems that often it is women who become the biggest obstacle to the placement of female pastors in congregations. Usually there are no specifics regarding the "concerns," only that there are "concerns" that this simply would not work. Why is it that women are taking on other women? No, not every female clergy is going to be the right fit for a congregation, but simply ruling out a woman because she is a woman is not right either, and maybe it's time to look at the motivation.

God has been calling women to be involved in his ministry for centuries. Who was it that carried the Messiah? Mary, the mother of Jesus, was asked to suffer the scorn and criticism of family members in order to bring Jesus into this world. Since the miraculous birth of Christ here on this earth Jesus has been calling women to be partners together with him in ministry. An entire team of women traveled with Jesus and the disciples during his years of ministry.

Is it possible that the most critical women in churches are those whom God had called, and for numerous circumstances or reasons did not respond to that calling? Now, instead of affirming women with a calling to ministry, we become "concerned" that it won't work. Why? Because her presence may be a constant reminder of the call that had been placed on our hearts! Sisters, it's time to ask God to forgive us if we didn't respond to the calling, move on, and stop taking it out on others in the sisterhood. The enemy knows that God's original plan for women was powerful, and he will do everything he can to destroy any alliances that may help restore women to the role God originally intended.

THE ISSUE OF APPEARANCE

Flipping through YouTube videos from *The Carol Burnett Show*, I was reminiscing about my high school days. I used to love that show and thought that Carol Burnett was probably the funniest and most talented woman I've ever seen. However, as I watched those forty-year-old videos something struck me about the appearance of the "stars" on the program. By today's standards they would seem incredibly ordinary, if not unattractive. What has happened to our society in the last forty years? We have become obsessed with beauty and youth, and this has certainly infiltrated the church.

A friend of mine shared with me a true story from a Sunday school class she attended a number of years ago. The peer pressure within that group of young adults led every single woman to have cosmetic breast surgery. Why would this happen? Because the message that women are receiving today from the world and from one another is that you are never going to be good enough. Instead of seeking God and the beauty found in Christ that is to be reflected in us, we look to the world for solutions. We are willing to hurt ourselves in an effort to adapt to some type of distorted view of the human body. The damage reaches beyond the bounds of our own flesh and touches those around us. That single Sunday school class probably spent a collective $100,000 in an effort to have "perky breasts." Just imagine what God could have done with that much money if it had been given to bring hope to women around the world who are simply looking to survive for another day.

Because we are busy measuring ourselves against the next woman, we sometimes ostracize sisters who desperately need our love and support, simply because of their looks. We probably think this is common with a woman who may not be as attractive as the next, but what happens when an attractive woman enters the room? First we look her over to determine whether or not she is for real, and second we look for the things we can criticize about her because in doing so we feel better about ourselves. Often this leaves the attractive woman as one of the loneliest people around, and surprisingly, with a poor self-image.

My husband, Chuck, went to a Christian college. His freshman year a beautiful girl who had worked as a professional model began to attend as well. Every boy in the college thought she was simply gorgeous. I'm guessing all the girls did as well. Sadly, she dropped out of school in her second semester because no one would talk to her. She never had a single date in college and left without becoming friends with the girls. How could that happen at a Christian institution?

No matter our appearance, it is important for each member of the sisterhood to become comfortable in her own skin. This was a part of the fall of humanity. Adam and Eve had been comfortable in the skin that God had created for them, but as soon as they sinned, they no longer wanted God to see them. They covered themselves up with makeshift clothing. No, I'm not advocating that we all walk around naked, but the restored woman needs to allow God to make her comfortable in her body. This is the body that God has given us, and God sees it as beautiful! Isn't that what matters? Therefore the sisterhood needs to be an affirming peer group. Realize that every woman needs encouragement and friendship as a member of the sisterhood.

Am I advocating that women do nothing to fix themselves up? No, I'm not suggesting that either, but we need to ask ourselves whether we are giving in to the pressure of society to do unnatural things to ourselves or to focus too much attention on our looks. There must be a balance!

THE MENTORING SISTER

As most women have, I've worn a number of different hats in my adult life. I've been a nurse, a mother, a wife, a daughter, a daughter-in-law, a pastor's wife, a missionary, a pastor, and a district superintendent, just to name a few. Along the way I've looked for other women to be examples, to show me how it's all supposed to be done. It wasn't until we were in our first pastorate in Austin, Texas, that I realized that the greatest female mentor in my life was my mother. She was the one who had "done it all." She had never believed that ministry was just my Dad's thing, but she had been the strong partner who had worked with him shoulder to shoulder throughout life. That's how I thought things were to be done. My mother was my mentor in my formative years.

The man sitting next to me was talking about a new mentoring program that he was helping to initiate in different locations around the country. The area in which he worked employed mostly men, and he said he'd run into a real problem. Most of the young people coming up through the ranks these days are female. He wasn't sure what to do with them because there weren't enough women in leadership positions who could mentor the sheer number of young ladies seeking mentors.

A recent study by LinkedIn showed that men tend to have more mentors in their lives than women.[3] Within the workforce this may have simply been the norm. The older "boss" generally takes the new young men in the office out to lunch or coffee, and mentoring begins to happen both formally and informally. To strengthen the sisterhood, women are going to need to be more intentional about mentoring other women. Women make excellent mentors because they tend to be very holistic.[4] Historically the role of older women was to train up the younger women. Somehow we have moved away from this and maybe it's time for us to once again pick up what has been lost and get back into the business of mentoring strong women. Young women need to actively seek out the more experienced women, and mature women need to recognize that their responsibility to the sisterhood includes mentoring the young women of our world.

THE ENCOURAGING SISTER

"Thelma, you did so well in therapy this morning. Good job!" "Mabel, I see you're walking with the walker now. That is just great." "Ardith, I saw you lifting weights today and you are just doing so well." My nearly ninety-year-old mother had just completed her third knee replacement, having outlived one of her artificial joints. Her hospital stay was followed by a week in a rehab facility where she would have to work hard to gain strength and flexibility in her leg. The routine included twice-daily visits to the physical therapy room where she would work through a series of sometimes excruciating exercises. While the pain made her uncomfortable, she was determined that she would gain back full range of motion and mobility. With a positive attitude and determination, she would wheel herself to her therapy session. Her room was near the end of the long corridor, and on her jaunt to therapy she would pass many other patients in their wheelchairs that were also there recovering. She worked hard to get to know the names of the other patients and every time she saw other patients she encouraged them. It was almost comical to listen as my mom, older than most of the other patients there, glided down the hallway and with a nod and a positive word pushed the others to continue on with their exercises.

My mother has been a positive influence for her entire life. She has always believed that with hard work and determination she could accomplish most anything. Along the way, she believed that with enough encouragement others could do the same, and so she never gave up on anyone.

"Alice, do you remember me?" My mother turned to look into the face of an attractive woman in her early sixties. My parents were attending a special worship service at a church in the neighboring town. Something in the face of this woman looked vaguely familiar, but my mother couldn't touch on it. Realizing my mom wasn't sure who she was, the woman recounted the following:

> My husband and I moved into the poor, rundown house next to your parsonage over forty years ago. You came over and talked to me and became my friend. Not only did you become my friend, but you also told me about Jesus. I've been serving

the Lord ever since. Alice, you taught me about life. You came and helped me clean my house. You taught me how to care for my home, and then you even taught me how to cook.

This woman had been transformed. She was still serving the Lord, having learned how to be a wife and a mother from the encouraging sister who lived next door.

I'm grateful for the heritage that I have received from my mother. Often people think they see my father in me, but that's just because they don't know my mom very well. She is an amazing woman who has taught me what it means to be an encouragement to the sisterhood, and I'm sure you'll believe me when I tell you that she has been my number one cheerleader throughout life.

"Doing, Mamma, doing?" My mother tells me that this was my favorite phrase when I was just a toddler, learning to walk and to talk. I would pull on my mother's skirt because I wanted to know what she was doing. She tells me that I wanted her to pick me up and put me on the kitchen counter so that I could be involved in whatever she was doing. I certainly didn't want to be left out. Throughout life she has reminded me about this and my favorite childhood phrase, "Doing, mamma?" My greatest cheerleader continues to encourage me in life. So often we don't know where life will lead. That is certainly true in my own life, and I'm not sure what all God has planned for the journey, but I know I want to be a faithful sister. My mother continues to watch my life and recently told me that now I'm holding onto the hem of Jesus' garment and asking, "Doing, God, doing?"

This is the picture of the encouraging sister and a reminder to all of us that we need to be supporting the sisterhood. We need a sister who will help us out in life and then point us in the direction of the Savior, saying now that I have encouraged you, let him lead you in all things.

Questions for Discussion

1. What is it that makes you feel the most uncomfortable about yourself?

2. What are practical ways that we can begin to build one another up?

3. What roles for women do we see as being more spiritual than others and why?

ASSIGNMENT

Commit to complimenting every sister you meet this week and report back about what happens.

4

"This is the covenant I will make with the people of Israel after that time," declares the LORD. *"I will put my law in their minds and write it on their hearts. I will be their God, and they will be my people."* (Jeremiah 31:33)

WHOLENESS

THE WOMAN AS OVERCOMER

I (Carla) had just moved to a new city—again! I was bracing myself for that first day at the new school. I hated it! Breathing deeply, I tried to push back the tears that I knew would come—they always did. The schedule for my classes had me going to band early in the day. Clutching my little black flute case tightly, I headed off to school. Who would I meet? Would I make new friends? Would they be friendly with me? My heart was pounding from the sheer terror of the experience.

The band room was filled with students who were milling around the room and finally making their way to their seats. I hung around the door, feeling conspicuous and wanting to melt into the walls. Mr. McClellan, the band director, stepped over to meet me. Immediately he welcomed me and made me feel at ease.[1] The metal folding chairs on the front row of the band were shuffled so that an additional seat could be placed at the end of the flute section. This was to be my new place in life, and I was happy to sink into oblivion in this position. Unfortunately, one of the most hated events of my life was scheduled for that day—seating tryouts! Stupidly, I decided that the best way to try and fit in was to participate, even though I didn't know the music. The problem was that I was pretty good at sight-reading and when I was terrified, I played at an incredibly rapid pace. The result could be deceptively impressive. Therefore when it was my turn I burned through the piece and there was an audible gasp from the group. In hindsight, I should have just passed that day. I was moved up to second chair and that brought with it the ire of the entire flute section. What a way to make friends on the first day! Sadly, I was afraid to allow anyone to see my flaws, and therefore I tried to overcompensate. I was afraid that I could never be perfect!

PERFECTION!

"Be perfect, therefore, as your heavenly Father is perfect" (Matthew 5:48). I would guess that for many, this verse brings a flood of emotion. For some reason this idea of being perfect has had a crippling effect on God's daughters, and yet there's something profound in this scripture.

As I was growing up, I really struggled with that verse. The idea of being perfect haunted me. I would go to church and listen to the preacher and think that the moment I walked out the door and made a mistake I was going to hell! I tried my best to be all that God wanted me to be, but perfection was simply a dream. The problem was that I was a shy and klutzy girl who didn't always do everything right. What I believed about this scripture and what I seemed to hear from different preachers was that I had to be a *perfect Christian*! This set me up for failure, for I could never meet that standard. But it affected the way I lived my life, including that first day of band class!

❧❧❧

As we have seen, women have a tendency to measure themselves against a particular standard, whether it's someone else or what we perceive to be the best model. I spend a portion of my time teaching adjunct at several universities, and I've learned that my students don't want me to grade them in any kind of a subjective manner. They want me to give them the grading rubric so that they have no doubt as to my expectation. If they know what the expectation is, then they know how to perform. There is comfort in knowing the expectation.

The problem with the Christian life is that we can't simply memorize a grading rubric for every possible situation we may encounter in life, therefore having a clear understanding of the behavioral expectation. The problem is that we are more comfortable with a list of expectations or a set of rules when it comes to living the Christian life. At least we *think* we are better at following a list, but when we look back to the children of Israel and their attempts at following the Ten Commandments, we discover how miserably they failed. Unfortunately, we humans tend to repeat history, and therefore our attempts at simply following a list of rules have also led us to failure.

For a number of years many churches attempted to define the Christian life by providing a list of rules. The problem with this is that the Christian life is about a relationship, and not about rules or a grading rubric for behavior. How many of us remember asking others about what their church believed, and by that question we were really asking about their list of rules? Did they go to movies? Did they dance? There seemed to be this idea that the stricter the rules, the holier those people must be. Perfect women must attend churches that have *really* good rules.

Some people who lived in Jesus' day thought this way. They were called Pharisees! They prided themselves on being very holy people who lived by a strict set of rules. They were proud of themselves and their ability to abide by the regulations, while at the same time coming up with all kinds of ways to get around the rules. There were instructions regarding a Sabbath day's journey. On the Sabbath day, they were to only travel about six-tenths of a mile from their home. This rule found its roots in the Old Testament during the time of Moses when the tabernacle was located about three-tenths of a mile outside the camp. Therefore you needed to travel this distance to worship the Lord and return home. By the time of Christ, the Pharisees had become fanatics regarding these rules that included instructions for only traveling this short distance on the Sabbath. Obviously the distance was quite restrictive to those who wanted to travel further. The Pharisees found a solution to this problem by placing personal belongings at the home of friends. These homes were strategically located a Sabbath day's journey from one another. In this way, they could call each of those homes "their home," and they could continue to travel a Sabbath day's journey from "their home." This allowed them freedom to cover a much larger area than they should have.

The Pharisees used to stroke themselves on the back, proud of the fact that they were being *perfect* followers of God by following all of the rules. At the same time they were blind to the Messiah's presence when he stood right in front of them. As much as we are uncomfortable with the comparison with the Pharisees, haven't there been times when we have comforted ourselves in the fact that we were good Christian girls because we were following the rules? If we were to be honest, haven't we also been like the Pharisees because we have looked for ways to get around the rules?

I remember when our church had a special rule that said that we couldn't go to movies. People were religious about not going to the movie theater, but these same people bought VCRs as soon as they became available so that they could "not go to the theater" but still watch the same movies in their homes. Somehow the real intent of the "rule" was lost and we became pharisaical in our observance of the rules. God knew this was our tendency, and through his prophet Jeremiah he prophesied about a new future that would come to fruition through the birth of the Messiah.

> "This is the covenant I will make with the people of Israel after that time," declares the Lord. "I will put my law in their minds and write it on their hearts. I will be their God, and they will be my people." (Jeremiah 31:33)

He was declaring the relational change that was to occur in the life of all humanity. Fallen sisters slip into the trap of following the rules because the relationship is distorted. The result is women trying in their own power to be perfect, but ending up frustrated. Is it any wonder that in many churches we have lost an entire generation or two of churchgoers who have simply said, "I can't be perfect" and "I find living by the rules unfulfilling"?

A DIFFERENT PERSPECTIVE ON PERFECTION

We have been talking a great deal about God's intention for his *ezers*, and the beauty that we find in their restoration. We have not spent much time talking about how that happens, and it relates directly to this idea of perfection. God has a plan for his perfected ones to be living here on this earth, but by now we may be wondering how that might be possible! God had a plan to breathe life back into those whom he had created in his image, both for the *adam* and the *ezer*. God's plan was to fill his people with his Holy Spirit, and in filling them with his Holy Spirit, he would transform their hearts, turning them around to face him and restoring their relationship with him and with one another. This meant that they would no longer live by a set of rules, but instead, they would be motivated by the desires of their heart, which would be to love God and love their neighbor. A true *ezer* is motivated by Christ and the desire for Christlikeness. Jesus becomes the very goal of her heart, and knowing him is what drives her to become the incredible woman that God intended her to be in the first place! She falls head over heels in love with Jesus.

It is the *ezer* in love with Jesus that then wrestles with understanding this command to be perfect. In our modern understanding, we see absolute perfection as existing without any flaws, imperfections, or mistakes, and we realize that we can never measure up to this standard, and yet our fears make us try.

We need to turn back the hands of time and take a look at what Jesus meant when he used the word "perfect." Jesus was a Jewish boy who was taught by Jewish principles and concepts, which meant he had a Hebrew understanding of the word "perfect." For him, if something were to be perfect, it would fulfill the purpose for which it was created. What were we created to be? Strong helpers, strong powers—*ezers*! Therefore, for God's daughters, to be perfect means that we are to reclaim the original Eve and be restored as God intended each one of us to be.

Living in Russia for a number of years I had the privilege of getting to know a number of God's women who taught me all kinds of new skills. It was one day while drinking a cup of Russian tea that God helped me understand what he really meant by being perfect. The women in the church had taught me how to make tea Russian-style, and the result was the best tea I had ever tasted. This wasn't just dropping a tea bag into some hot water. For a *real* cup of tea, there was a procedure to be followed. Water must be heated to boiling. After the water is boiling hot it is poured into a tiny pot called a zavarka. This zavarka is usually about one-third full of wonderfully aromatic tea leaves. One had to allow the tea to steep in the zavarka until it was very strong and potent. Next, some of the concentrated hot tea from the zavarka would be poured into a teacup. More or less tea from the zavarka would determine the strength of the tea and then the cup would be filled to the brim with more boiling hot water. At this point, you could sit down at the table with your friends and enjoy sipping that perfect cup of tea.

Sounds good, doesn't it? I'm relaxing with that kitchen conversation, but wait a minute—let's really examine that cup of tea. Why would we call it perfect? The china in Russia wasn't very fancy, in some ways even thick and heavy, and the cup was a little old. If you examined the cup closely, you would find a small chip around the lip. When I poured from the zavarka, some leaves slipped into the cup as well. The leaves weren't all of uniform size or shape. However, I'm still willing to call it a perfect cup of tea. Why is that? Because the tea fulfilled the purpose for which it was made. It tasted so good. It warmed me up. I am no longer thirsty. I have been satisfied. This is the Hebrew understanding of perfection.

So, then, how are we to be perfect, as our "heavenly Father is perfect" (Matthew 5:48)? It's not perfect on the outside, but rather, it's becoming all that he intended for us to be, and that meant we were to be in a relationship with Christ that includes reflecting his love to the world.

THE PERFECTED SISTER

The description of Eve before the fall is rather brief, and therefore we don't have a lot of information about how she lived her life as the *ezer* God had intended. What we do know is that the main feature of her life was that she was created in the image of God. As we continue studying the Scriptures, we begin to understand more and more of God's nature, and this reveals to us what the strong helper is supposed to be like. Why? Because the strong helper is a reflection of the nature of God. This means that perfection comes when we successfully reflect Christ to the world around us.

Standing in the dressing room, I was looking at myself in the three-way mirror. Or shall we call it the "rear-view" mirror? As much as I hate seeing myself in this kind of mirror, there is something fun about being able to see everything from so many different angles. The dress I was trying on had very tiny details at the bottom. The closer I stood to the mirror, the more I could see the detail work and the beauty of the garment. As I moved and shifted, the dress moved and shifted with me, and I saw a true reflection of the garment in action. Jesus is living and active and moving in our world today, and a true *ezer* not only looks like Christ but acts and moves like Christ as well!

Restored sisters overflow with love from the Father that splashes out on the world around us. Because we are all unique and special in God's eyes, to be a perfect reflection of Christ looks different for each one of us. That's the beauty. We are not to be compared to one another.

Each will express her love relationship to Christ in a different way. Some might experience God calling them into specific types of ministry. For a young lady named Jonnie, the call of God meant that she was to go into full-time ministry with her husband. Mrs. Jonnie Jernigan became an early leader and minister in what was known as the "holiness movement." I can imagine her dressed in dark, conservative clothing with long sleeves and a high neckline—yet she went to surprising locations, called to reflect Christ by loving young women who had fallen into a life of sin. She wrote about God's work in her life:

> I am glad that God has given me a mother's heart and a mother's love for poor, erring girls; and it is my delight to go into the haunts of shame and hunt them up and lead them back to a life of purity. It seems that so little has been done by the churches of our day to rescue the fallen and bring them back to a life of virtue. As I look out on the white harvest field of over-ripe grain, and see the few willing workers who are reaping the harvest, my heart bleeds at every pore, and I hear the sad wails and sobs of some mother's poor, unfortunate girl, as she lies dying in a haunt of shame, with no one to pity or to help her.

> I have done what little I could since I consecrated my life to God and He sanctified me. . . Now, my constant prayer to God is that He may raise up many mothers and maids to carry on this great work of lifting up the fallen and bringing them back to a life of respectability.[2]

Jonnie Jernigan's ministry to young women in the brothels continued for a number of years. Eventually she opened an orphanage for the babies born to so many of these young ladies. Jonnie was not caught up in the externals of life, but rather, on being one who reflected God's love to a hurt and dying world. In this, she fulfilled the purpose for which God had created her and she was *perfect.*

This is the good news. It is possible to be an *ezer* today, fulfilling our God-given purpose in the world. But many of us are so terribly wounded that this dream may seem a distant reality. We may feel as far removed from being an *ezer* as we do from Eve herself. How do we, as wounded women, find this wholeness?

THE WOUNDED SISTER

Deandra arrived at her very first day of college. She was excited about the new world that lay in front of her, and she was ready to put her past behind. Those thoughts from her childhood were too painful to remember. Her parents didn't know anything about what had happened in the safety of their Christian home. Her mother's brother had come to live with them when Deandra was just eight years of age. Often at the dinner table she would catch him staring at her in a way that made her uncomfortable. She wasn't sure why, but she just knew that something didn't feel right, and yet her parents had told her to do all she could to welcome Uncle David into the home.

David was in need of the Lord and as a family they thought they might be able to minister to him. What her parents didn't know was that at night Uncle David was sneaking into Deandra's bedroom. She didn't know why he was coming to her room, but she thought she'd better be nice so that he could get to know Jesus. Without saying a word he slipped into bed beside her and then began to slowly put his hand in places that no one had ever touched. She was terrified, and yet never said anything, afraid that her parents would be disappointed in her if she messed things up for Uncle David. Night after night she would lie in bed terrified, listening intently, trying to discern whether it was the tick-tock of the grandfather clock echoing off the tile floor of the hallway or the footsteps of Uncle David coming to her room.

Finally Uncle David moved on, but not until after Deandra had been thoroughly scarred and shamed. No longer was her home a haven, but a place that she hoped to escape. College was going to set her free!

Every year Christian universities are filled with young women arriving with the same dream as Deandra—to be set free. Shockingly a university counselor recently told me that 25 percent of incoming freshmen girls at Christian universities report to their resident assistant that a family member has molested them in the home. If this many open up and share this information, just imagine how many don't say a word. That means that there are thousands of Deandras out there who are the walking wounded. They are angry at their parents and at the church. Poor self-images run rampant and the overcompensation runs the gamut of dressing provocatively to prove that men really do like them, to overeating and becoming purposely overweight to repel men by creating a protective barrier, to an obsession with perfection. Through the years the ingrown hurt creates an intense energy that is often expressed as a critical spirit that lashes out at others in an effort to make oneself feel better. The desire for perfection actually drives us into destructive behaviors.

The world is filled with wounded women who put on a tough front to protect their hearts from the deep-seated hurts that life has inflicted. As God's women, we are invited to link arms with our injured sisters and to be their strong helpers, picking them up and helping them see that Jesus can heal their wounds.

HEALING AND WHOLENESS FOR THE WOUNDED SISTER

For years she was embarrassed to leave the house. Her period had started twelve years ago and had never gone away. Some days it was worse than others, accompanied by debilitating cramps and heavier bleeding. There were no medications that would alleviate that awful pain deep in her belly, and she would double over with every sharp stab. It was the first century and there were no store shelves filled with feminine hygiene products. Instead she had been washing rags out for years, and the entire world knew that she was "unclean." She had hoped the doctors could help her, and most of the money she was able to scrape together was spent on medical assistance. Unfortunately, treatment didn't make her any better; she simply became worse.

Her husband left her because he realized that she was unable to bear children. Alone and frightened in this world, one day she decided to do something that just might change everything. She had heard that a man named Jesus was coming to town. He was a rabbi, a great teacher, but he was also performing miracles. This was her last hope, and she truly believed that he could take away this terrible affliction.

The crowds were pressing in around this man, Jesus. Knowing she was unclean, she felt conspicuous making her way through the throng. Surely they must have all known that she had no business being there. If only she could sneak in and simply touch his clothing, she was sure that his power would heal her. Reaching her hand between the people crowding around Jesus, she grasped his clothing between her fingers for a brief moment. In that instant, something happened. She felt the power of God course through her very being, and immediately the bleeding stopped. Wanting to run away before anyone could catch her there among the people, she stopped dead in her tracks when Jesus called out, "Who touched my clothes?"

The disciples were stunned that Jesus would ask such a question when obviously many people had touched him, but Jesus knew that someone had touched him with the very purpose of being healed. He had felt the power surge from his body into someone else. Shaking from fear and barely able to walk, she fell before Jesus and told him the whole story. In gentleness he reached out to her and every gospel account tells us that he called her "daughter." He affirmed this woman as one of his children within the kingdom of God. She was not an outcast; she was a child of the King. Not only was she healed physically, but the original word may also be translated to mean "whole." Everything that had been turned upside down in her world because of her illness was now set right and she was a daughter within God's kingdom. She had now been made perfect.[3]

RESTORATION AND WHOLENESS FOR WOMEN

We have to ask ourselves why this story shows up in three of the gospel accounts, because not all stories do! Obviously there was something overwhelmingly unique about this story that the gospel writers knew and understood. Jesus' behavior was radical when it came to ministering to women. He seemed to continually turn the world upside down with his actions, and this story is one of those cases. This is not just the story of one woman, but it is the story of all women. From the time that Eve sinned in the garden, women bore the burden of guilt that manifested itself in actually being a woman! What distinguishes women more than their monthly cycle? God had predicted that women would have pain in childbirth, and the monthly period had become a regular reminder of that pain. In the Old Testament, blood sacrifices were given on a regular basis to make people clean, but in the case of women, it was their monthly cycles that made them unclean. The very thing that normally purified people made women dirty. This woman reached out in faith and touched Jesus' clothing and she was immediately healed. Her impurity did not make Jesus unclean; instead, his power and holiness poured over her body. Not only was she healed physically, but she was also made whole again. She represents Eve, the woman who has suffered for so long for being a woman, and her story is purposefully included so that we understand that Jesus came to set things right again, to make this woman whole again, and to make all women who may think that they are damaged whole again, to bring them to perfection!

This brings us back to linking arms with our sisters. Some of our sisters need help making it through the crowd and reaching out to touch Jesus. They need a strong woman to lift them up from where they are and make a way for them to get to Jesus. The wounded and damaged sisters represent a hidden sin of our world today. Gender-based violence is a horrible crime that is swept under the rug. Whether the violence manifests itself in young women growing up in "Christian" homes or girls being sold into the sex trade in Asia, we need to be a voice for those who have none. An *ezer* fights injustice while beating a path to Jesus for those who need his healing touch.

THE *EZER* OVERCOMES

We come full circle as we return to this idea of perfection. I know that I will never be a perfect flute player in this lifetime. There are many things that I will never do perfectly from a human perspective, but I do believe that I can reclaim Eve and become the strong power and strong helper that God wants me to be, and we have seen that this hope exists for every woman, no matter how wounded. Jesus knows about our hidden secrets and he says not to worry; he is powerful enough to bring healing and restore us.

I mentioned earlier that we would discuss *how* this might be possible. For every person the *how* may look a little different. Before Jonnie could even imagine being a strong helper to the wounded women around her, she had to get her own act together! Jonnie mentioned that she had consecrated her life to God and that he had sanctified her. The Christian life is a journey that begins the day you ask Christ into your life. It's as if you step back in front of that big three-way mirror, only you're about twenty feet away and the reflection is really small. Every day of that journey, we continually move closer to the original image by way of spiritual formation so that the reflection begins to fill up the entire frame and the beautiful one that God created is visible to the world. Along the journey there come moments where we discover that we have major obstacles in our path that are keeping us from being the complete reflection that God had intended. There may be boulders of woundedness in our lives that are blocking the flow of the Holy Spirit into every corner of our being. Sometimes these boulders create a very real crisis in our lives, and we realize that if they are not removed they will forever obscure the reflection of

Christ in our lives. For him to entirely fill us, we must be willing to offer up the boulders to him and in doing so, we will discover that being the strong power he intended is much easier than we ever thought.

This is what the prophet Jeremiah was talking about. God knew that his people could not simply follow a list of rules in their own power. Instead, Christlikeness had to be restored into their very nature. Only by being an *ezer* can a woman be perfect, for that was what God created her to be. Being an *ezer* means that she doesn't follow a list of rules; she simply fulfills the purpose for which God made her and surprisingly the rules are followed. And now we can breathe a collective sigh of relief!

Only through the power of the Holy Spirit can we live the life that God has intended. It's not just a matter of will. The woman with the twelve-year period didn't will away the bleeding. Her will got her to where Jesus was, but then it was the power that was present in Christ that poured through every corner of her being that brought complete and total wholeness to her life. Our responsibility is to come willingly before him, but then allow the Holy Spirit to empower us to live the life God intended for us.

If you are satisfied to simply live by a set of rules, you don't know what it means to be set free by the power of his Holy Spirit! The greatest obstacle to allowing the Holy Spirit to entirely fill you and transform you into his *ezer* is *you*!

MY JOURNEY

As I said before, there is no one set path for climbing higher or closer to Christ. Each of us is on her own journey that is unique to each and every one of God's creations. My own crisis experience came when I had been following Christ for a number of years. The time came when I would need to make plans for my future. I had my own ideas about what I wanted to accomplish in life and what I wanted to study. All of them were good things, nothing evil. Believe it or not, I wanted to study music! Yes, I was still playing that flute, as well as a few other instruments, and singing. However, this was not what it meant for me to be God's *ezer,* and it became more and more clear to me as I was preparing to enter college. While I had planned to major in music, little by little I knew that God was speaking to me about going into nursing. The problem was that I didn't want to study nursing. I couldn't even stand the sight of blood! I reminded the Lord that I had passed out in high school biology class trying to do a blood test on myself and any ideas about nursing were simply ridiculous!

For months I ignored the voice of God and continued with my personal plans for the future. Interestingly, at this time I'd been having conversations with my mother about wanting to go deeper in my Christian walk. I was seeking to understand what it meant to be a young *ezer.* Somehow I didn't put it together that this struggle was not simply about going into nursing but was a struggle over who was going to be in control of my life! Was I going to be a restored *ezer*? Yes, I could be a Christian and do good things for him, but then what kind of an *ezer* would I be? Would I be half an *ezer*? Would I allow him to have ultimate control of everything in my life? I wasn't sure. I didn't know if I could trust him. I still wanted to be in control. I was creating my own obstacles to reflecting Christ.

After months of wrestling with God there came an evening where God's presence became almost palpable. I was at a camp in St. Simon's Island, Georgia, at a place where John Wesley had once walked called Epworth by the Sea. That night I sat in the darkness beside the water, listening as the waves lapped up on the inky black rocks of the shore. Suddenly it was as if I could imagine Jesus on the seashore making breakfast for his disciples. The scene played out in front of me as Jesus took Peter by the hand and asked him whether he truly loved him! It was at that moment that I realized that I did not truly love Jesus. I had not been willing to hand all of my future over to him, nor had I been willing to put all of my trust in him. I was trying hard to make a go of it on my own. As I prayed that night, I finally allowed all of my fears and anxieties about my life to be moved over onto him. I relinquished control of my life into God's hands and told him that I would do whatever he desired for me to do. At that moment, such a sense of peace washed over me, and I sensed God in a way I never had before. It was as if I had opened every crevice of my life to the filling of God's Holy Spirit.

I returned to my room that evening and opened my Bible to spend some time in the Word. My Bible fell open to Habakkuk, not a common place for me to be reading. There the Lord led me to these words: "Look at the nations and watch—and be utterly amazed. For I am going to do something in your days that you would not believe, even if you were told" (Habakkuk 1:5). If God would have told me that night that the Berlin Wall would eventually come down and that I would be sent as a missionary behind that wall, I would not have believed him. However, I believe that was part of God's plan for my life and he needed a young lady to be an *ezer*, to be willing to answer his call, to help prepare for the years that would lie ahead.

As a young woman, I went off to college to study nursing. There was some confusion regarding roommate assignments and into my room walked Judy, whom I had never met. "I've just been diagnosed with diabetes," Judy mentioned right after the introductions. "I'm still trying to figure out what that means for me and how to keep my blood sugar stable." Together, we as roommates learned many a lesson on how to keep her levels stable, but

I struggled with watching her give herself twice-daily injections of insulin. I would literally hide my eyes, afraid that I would get sick just from seeing the needle. "God, why would you call me to be a nurse?" Little by little, Judy helped me overcome my fears and soon we were sneaking grapefruit out of the cafeteria so she could help me practice giving injections. Finally by the end of the year, I was able to prepare and give her injections without it even bothering me. God even cares about empowering a young, scared *ezer* when she is willing to be his reflection to the world.

Years later as I stood in Red Square I was in awe of the journey on which God had taken me. What was I doing behind the Berlin Wall? God had taken my husband and me to a place where we were able to minister in his name by virtue of the fact that we had humanitarian visas, and that I was a registered nurse. I continue to grow, trying to faithfully draw closer to him each day, but I only know that it's possible through his power.

Are you still trying to follow a list to be perfect? You will never be good enough if that is the kind of perfection you are seeking for your life. You can never be an *ezer* by following a rulebook, nor can you heal yourself from the woundedness of life. Allow God to write his desires on your heart and then allow him to make you as beautiful and perfect as he can imagine. It doesn't happen overnight, but it is the beginning of a journey that will last until the day you finally get so close to Christ, the original image, that you will see him face-to-face. It is in walking the Spirit-filled journey that you will experience *real* Christian perfection as an overcomer, reclaiming Eve and becoming a beautiful *ezer*!

Questions for Discussion

1. When you read or hear the word "perfect," what feelings come to mind?

2. What have you observed people doing to get around "church rules"?

3. Woundedness exists all around us—what types of woundedness have you encountered? What are you doing to address these needs?

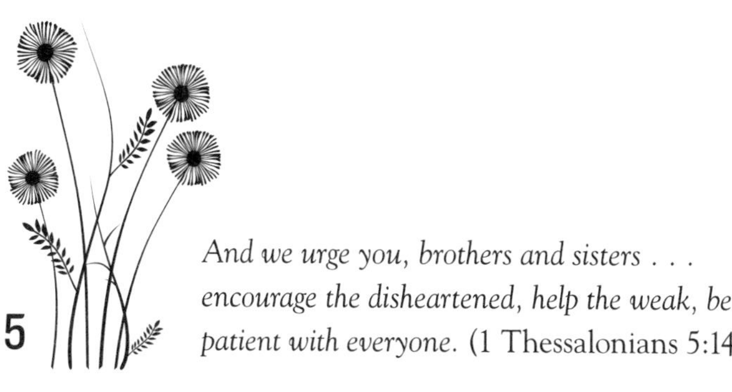

5

And we urge you, brothers and sisters . . .
encourage the disheartened, help the weak, be
patient with everyone. (1 Thessalonians 5:14)

HEALING

RESTORED IN COMMUNITY

"I was set free from pornography," he said, with feeling in his voice. I (Suzanne) blinked, looked back at him and surveyed the rest of the Bible fellowship class. "And how did that happen, Jim?" I asked gently. "Did you find an accountability partner or a software program?" He looked me squarely in the eyes and said, "Jesus Christ."

I'll admit—I think I gasped a little. Sadly, it's not often that someone in church admits his or her struggle with pornography. Jim explained that two weeks after accepting Christ, he gladly deleted all four hundred images off his computer and replaced them with Christian music. Unbelievable.

In the weeks and months that followed, I began to notice a pattern in Jim's life. As Jim interacted with the community around him, he willingly shared his weaknesses and his brokenness before God with the class. We often noticed tears in his eyes as he shared with the group how he longed for his wife to attend church with him or for his father to come to know the Lord. He admitted wrongdoing and asked for prayer. Gently, Jim would confront others, always looking for ways to serve them. And he regularly received the comfort, insight, and consolation of those who loved him.

I have watched as Jim, the new believer, has taught those of us who have been in the church our whole lives how to truly live in Christ-centered community. If only the church—and every person who follows Jesus—could learn from his example.

THE LONGING FOR COMMUNITY

The spirit of our times could be described with one word: "alienation." Garage doors go down, people sit entranced in front of computers and televisions, while the solitary lives we lead are crushing our souls. There isn't a person God will put in your path today who doesn't long to be known and loved. The bank teller, the boss, the mail carrier, the child, the client, the sister, the old college roommate who just asked to be your Facebook friend.

If it's true that God calls to us in our pain, then he calls to the isolated businesswoman who has no friend to call when she needs to visit the emergency room. With arms outstretched, he beckons the teenager who was just rejected by her boyfriend after being used. He patiently longs to comfort the fifty-year-old woman whose father abandoned her at birth, leaving a gaping emotional wound that paralyzes her in relationships.

We all long for connection. The *ezers* and the *adams*. The single and the married. Those with power and money and those with nothing. In fact, a study from the University of Chicago showed that as you age, loneliness actually raises your blood pressure just as much as obesity or a lack of exercise.[1] The message: healing is a group activity. It's not only unfulfilling but also physically dangerous to go it alone.

We were hardwired for community. And while you may not have thought about it in this way, you've known it all along. You knew it when your mother or father laid you down as an infant and you longed to be held. You may remember moments of friendship that made your heart soar, along with your confidence. And if you're anything like me, you remember a time when your body physically ached from the ending of a relationship you held dear.

How amazing that in a world of isolated individuals, God the Creator provides the answer to our longings by pointing us back to his original plan. Remember? A God of community, dancing around in a three-in-one relationship, creates Adam. Immediately afterward, he recognizes Adam's loneliness, highlighting Adam's complete lack of any suitable companion. Then God dispenses a prescription with only glorious side effects: *to end the loneliness of the single human, I will make an* ezer *who is suitable for him.*

The Creator who made his *ezers* designed them as agents of rescue to destroy isolation. Think of it: simply by being born female, you are a dazzling testament to the beauty of community. You see, it is not good for Adam, or for anyone, to be alone. It violates God's design and leaves us empty, depressed, and even hopeless. God created his *ezers* to remind us over and over again that we cannot, *must not*, go it alone.

At the most basic level, even the storybook characters of our childhood reminded us of what our hearts already yearned for:

> Piglet sidled up to Pooh from behind. "Pooh?" he whispered.
>
> "Yes, Piglet?"
>
> "Nothing," said Piglet, taking Pooh's paw. "I just wanted to be sure of you."[2]

COMMUNITY GONE WRONG

I guess we've made it perfectly obvious that the first sin dealt a deathblow to our relationships. The perfect union the God of oneness had created fractured with a snap, leading Adam and Eve to a painful discovery: *When I sin against God, I will sin against others.*

Can you imagine? The Adam meant to cleave to Eve would rule over her by his own power and physical strength. The *ezer* designed to rescue the *adam* from loneliness would be frustrated, longing for something more from the one she was to rescue and rule with. They were naked. They knew it. And no one was sorrier than the Creator who had built them to thrive in relationship with one another.

❧❧❧

"I don't have anyone left," said Katie, tears streaming down her face as she gradually emptied the box of tissues on my desk. "If God loves me, why does he take everyone away from me?"

Why indeed, I thought. Katie had been shuffled from foster home to foster home. Not surprisingly, she found her adult years peppered with a slough of broken relationships. And now, as Katie tried to nurture a relationship with God while taking her kids to church, a lengthy relationship with another man had ended, stealing her dreams for the future.

I was most afraid of the wall she was erecting around herself, isolating her and her kids from any hope of meaningful community. Katie's heart was breaking from rejection and abandonment, and I knew that any hope of healing could only come from Jesus and those who follow him. There was only one thing that could revive Katie's heart so it could beat with hope again: really believing the truth that Jesus loves her and is for her, and experiencing that love through those called to be his hands and feet. This would require an openness Katie did not currently possess.

And so I asked her to do something as the tears rolled on. "Katie, will you put your hands down and clench them? Your fingernails are digging into your hands, aren't they? This is us trying to live controlling our lives. Now turn your hands up, opening them and surrendering to Jesus and all that he wants to give you." But Katie found she couldn't physically hold her hands open. "My hands are clenched," she said. "And besides that, my arms are crossed."

COMMUNITY GONE RIGHT AGAIN

How ironic that the very place in which Adam and Eve violated God's love is the place in which he wants to restore each of us. His community. The place in which each of us are hurt the most, through our relationships, happens to be the same avenue in which God wants to bring unimaginable healing. Whether or not you like it, you, like Katie, are dependent on other men and women to fully experience Christ's love for you.

I once had an acquaintance tell me he was getting everything he needed to know about God by watching church on television. This is the same guy who, by God's mercy, ended up attending my church, participating in a Bible class, making friendships, and eventually marrying someone he met at church. He and his wife are raising their kids in the same church today. Ask him again and he'll tell you: solo Christianity doesn't work, because it's not the way God designed it.

In Genesis 3:15, we read that because of their sin, Adam and Eve will experience "enmity" or "hatred" between them. But the same verse makes a reference to God's eventual plan to turn things right side up again. The seed of the woman (Jesus) would bruise the head of the serpent that had deceived them. The hope of community would be restored, and it would happen through the life, death, and resurrection of Jesus Christ.

Dealing his own deathblow to solo Christianity, Jesus prayed for you in John 17:

> I pray also for those who will believe in me through their message, that all of them may be one, Father, just as you are in me and I am in you. May they also be in us so that the world may believe that you have sent me. I have given them the glory that you gave me, that they may be one as we are one—I in them and you in me—so that they may be brought to complete unity. Then the world will know that you sent me and have loved them even as you have loved me. (Vv. 20-23)

Do you understand now that according to Jesus there is no plan B? The Bible tells us:

1. God, within the Trinity, created humans to be in community.
2. He sustains community as the Holy Spirit works in the lives of individual believers to bring them together as one.

3. The gospel itself—the message of freedom in Christ for all eternity—will only be known and shared through this same community.

The truth is, Jesus came to redeem and restore the community that was lost when Adam and Eve sinned. As outrageous as it seems, we are God's plan to bring healing and wholeness back to his creation. God's Word says he has "committed to us the message of reconciliation" (2 Corinthians 5:19). Look in the mirror, then look around you: you and others are designed to be loving agents of reconciliation in God's redemptive plan.

❧❧❧

"He really must love me," Katie said the last time we met. She shared how she had sinned against God in her isolation, but how her heavenly Father had protected her from further sin and hurt. "When I came to you I was at the end of myself, and I didn't see how I could go on," Katie said. "Now I know that God loves me and that he does want good for me."

I saw myself in Katie, remembering so many times when depression, loneliness, and abandonment had kept me locked in shame. "And what about your hands, Katie?" I asked. "Are they clenched still, or are they open to receive all your heavenly Father longs to give you?"

"I am working on that," she said. "And it is slowly getting easier to hold them open." I smiled and told her she would need some help to keep working on that—that God has provided his church to help her.

THE PROMISE OF COMMUNITY

Wouldn't it be great to live in perfect community, just like the Trinity? No petty squabbles to negotiate; no hurt feelings, betrayal, or abuse to recover from; no misunderstandings or words that one would rather take back. Just mutual giving and receiving, loving and being loved, knowing intimately and being intimately known. Now that would be heavenly.

And, of course, this is just the ending God has already written to his story, to all of history. The plan of redemption and reconciliation is underway; the fracture is already being healed by the blood of Jesus; the end of the story will bring a harmony to our relationships that we can only dream about. As we join hands together today, we look to a tomorrow filled with pure fellowship, unhindered oneness, and holy love:

> I saw the Holy City, the new Jerusalem, coming down out of heaven from God, prepared as a bride beautifully dressed for her husband. And I heard a loud voice from the throne saying, "Look! God's dwelling place is now among the people, and he will dwell with them. They will be his people and God himself will be with them and be their God." (Revelation 21:2-3)

God's Word goes on to say that death and mourning and crying will be gone—removed—and the old way of doing things will be done away with forever (Revelation 21:4). Hallelujah! Those who follow Christ make up this New Jerusalem, this dazzling bride waiting for her faithful husband. And the image of God as our future groom only makes our heart beat faster: for as everyone knows with a wink and a nod, the bride and the groom must be together. Their burning desire for each other cannot be quenched. Their love and longing for oneness must be consummated; their hearts will beat as one. This perfect oneness, displayed so beautifully through the image of a bride and a bridegroom is God's promise, and it is every Christian's sure and certain hope.

So, is it just me, or is this what it feels like to be seated in a cosmic waiting room? For we are the bride in waiting. We are the ones dreaming of perfect fellowship with God and others. We are the ones waiting for the show to go on. But in another sense, we are not waiting at all. Instead, we are working. We are charged with working to build the kingdom of Jesus in the here and now. Out of the wreckage of Adam and Eve's sin came the promise of a new community initiated by a Jewish carpenter, his bloody cross, and what can only be described as a miraculous resurrection.

NEW CREATION, NEW COMMUNITY

"We were therefore buried with him through baptism into death in order that, just as Christ was raised from the dead through the glory of the Father, we too may live a new life" (Romans 6:4).

Ever wonder what the women at the tomb were thinking the morning they discovered it empty? Clearly, Mary Magdalene thought someone had stolen the body: "They have taken the Lord out of the tomb, and we don't know where they have put him!" (John 20:2). I imagine great tears of sorrow and thoughts like these: *It wasn't enough to crucify our Master in front of us? The Romans have already crushed our hearts—now they are cutting them out and stomping on them as well.*

Gratefully, the depth of the women's pain would be no match for the joy soon to erupt. For the first undeniable sign of this new community would be a Savior who was very much alive. It wasn't the empty tomb that gave Mary Magdalene hope again; it was the voice of the very much alive Jesus that made her physically jump for joy. And the fact that he appeared first to her signaled a dramatic departure from relationships as usual. For as a woman in her culture, Mary Magdalene held few rights. She would never hold up as an official eyewitness to anything in court. She was likely aware that the pious male Jews thanked God regularly that they were not born as women. She knew her place, and her place would always be second.

Apparently Jesus did not get the memo. After what historians point to as the pivotal events in all of human history—Christ's death and resurrection—Jesus chose to appear not to his circle of male disciples, but to a female disciple who loved and served him faithfully. And he told her to immediately go and tell the twelve male disciples. What is so terribly ironic in all of this is that none of them believed her (Mark 16:11). Yet Mary would go down in history as "the apostle to the apostles"—the one chosen by Jesus to spread the good news.

Over time, this band of believers would begin to realize the significance of Jesus' death in leveling the playing field. At the foot of the cross, women were suddenly equal to men. The poor were just as blessed—if not more so—than the rich. Those perceived to be insignificant were accepted and just as desirable as the most powerful rulers in the world. The cross displayed a new way of being and relating. For as Christ accepts us (see the vertical bar), we are to accept one another (horizontal bar). At the intersection of the cross, true community was re-created. And not just for a fortunate few: "There is neither Jew nor Gentile, neither slave nor free, nor is there male and female, for you are all one in Christ Jesus" (Galatians 3:28).

Vertical—Christ accepts us.
Horizontal—we accept one another.[3]

~~~

She tore off a hunk of bread from the Communion loaf and carefully dunked it in the cup I held. "Kitty," I said. "The body of
~~~

Christ was broken for you, and his blood was spilled out for you." Her reply brought a smile to my face and a sting to my heart. "For me?" she said out loud. "Well, I don't know why, but if you say so." And then the bread and the juice slid down her throat, the spirit of Christ's sacrifice lingering in the air, the reminder of the body and the blood uniting our small group as one.

For if we were honest, each one taking Communion that morning could have said the same. Though none of us was worthy, Christ died for us. In a stunning show of power and authority, he rose from the dead. He will return for his bride someday. In the meantime, there is a sense in which "happily ever after" has already arrived. For, although all is not yet perfect, we can begin to lay hold of the beautiful promise of community restored. And that is exactly what Jesus invites us to:

> As I have loved you, so you must love one another. By this everyone will know that you are my disciples, if you love one another. (John 13:34-35)

HEALING THROUGH COMMUNITY

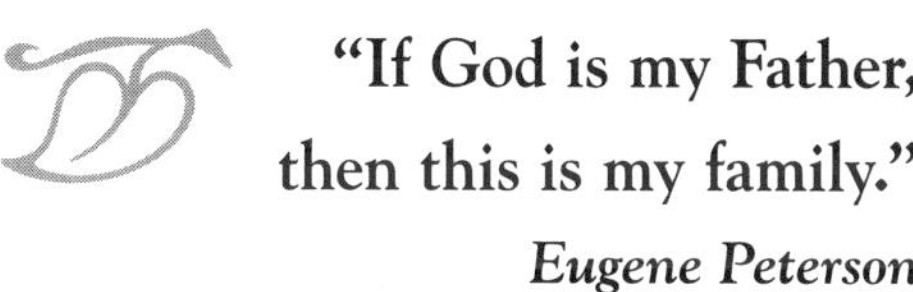

"If God is my Father, then this is my family."
Eugene Peterson

Sunday morning in church I sat happily sandwiched in the middle of an unlikely crew. I wish you could have seen our faces. On my left sat my newly believing friend, Adrienne, the one I am helping to disciple, the one who got baptized just last spring. I remember helping to dunk her under the water, and the way she came up, sparkling and clean, smiling and whole. To her left sat our beautiful white-haired friend, Jane, whom the world calls special, her innocence breaking out in dance when the songs begin. My husband, David, smiled contentedly on my right. And on his other side our friend Jim snuck in, the one who winsomely inspires community, the one I mentioned at the start of the chapter.

Dazzled by the beauty of it all, all I could think was: *Lord, your body inspires joy. Your vision for community makes me want to sing. In this family, each of us belongs.* The more I study the New Testament and the mission of Jesus, the more I become convinced that his view of family provides the only way to true healing through community. In fact, if Jesus were preaching a sermon on community at your church next Sunday, his message might shock your ears.

For after joyfully welcoming the broken and the bedraggled, he might say, "I want to remind you that in my kingdom, you're not required to come to church with your biological family. In my body, we make up our own family. I am your brother. You are my sister. If God is our Father, this is our family."

Make no mistake, Jesus valued the institution of marriage, and he certainly valued his own mother. But when pressed to define his "first family," he made statements like these: "Whoever does God's will is my brother and sister and mother" (Mark 3:35). In John 19, as he hung on the cross, he told his mother, Mary, that John was now her son, and that she was now his mother. The spiritual family trumped the physical family. Neither being single nor being married was a determiner of status in God's kingdom—for whatever lot in life one was called to, believers in Jesus formed an automatic family. As one author has rightly pointed out, "There are no single Christians."[4]

WOMEN RESTORED IN COMMUNITY

My Bible lay open on my knees as our recovery Bible study picked up steam. "In the Old Testament, priests had to offer sacrifices to God to atone for sins," I said. "But when Jesus came, he became our sacrifice. Now the Bible says we are all priests, that we can approach God directly."

"Women too?" she asked, with genuine surprise on her face.

"Yes!" I said, more loudly than was necessary, as my heart plummeted to the ground.

❧❧❧

"But you are . . . a royal priesthood . . . that you may declare the praises of him who called you out of darkness into his wonderful light" (1 Peter 2:9). My Bible study friend needed assurance that God's promise to men was also God's promise to women. I've been there myself. And if you were honest, perhaps you would say you're still looking for some reassurance too. That would put you in good company with the women in the New Testament, women whose social and spiritual standing was suddenly upended by the gospel of Jesus Christ.

Under the new community Jesus created through the cross and resurrection, women were set free in ways they could hardly have imagined. Women in the early church who were widowed and destitute had their needs provided for by their spiritual family. Believers ate together daily and "had everything in common" (Acts 2:44). The women, who were previously denied simple rights and were often treated as property, became ministers of God's amazing grace. That explains the clear break in Jewish tradition as the New Testament commends Phoebe the deacon, Priscilla the teacher, Dorcas the disciple, and Junia the apostle. The old had gone, and the new had clearly arrived.

How amazing, then, that two thousand years later so many Christian women are unsure of what their place should be. In the last several decades, there has been a push for evangelical women to return to "God's vision for the family." To put it bluntly, as we've pointed out, some have insisted that the highest calling of a biblical woman is to be a wife and mother. It actually sounds admirable, except for the fact that Jesus is not calling all women to be wives and mothers and that he actually commends singleness. Then there's the fact that Jesus proclaimed to every male and female that their highest calling, the greatest commandment of all, was to love the Lord their God with all of their heart, soul, mind, and strength and their neighbor as themselves (Matthew 22:37-39). He commissioned men and women to love him, love others, and to spread the gospel through the whole world, teaching others to live the Jesus way (Matthew 28:16-20).

Let me be clear: the highest calling on any woman's life is to love the Lord her God with all of her heart, to love her neighbor as she loves herself, and to take the good news of Jesus to the world. While I am sorry if this news comes as a shock to you, I would be more sorry if I didn't point out what Jesus is asking of each of us. We can be single, divorced, married or remarried, mothers or not, employed outside the home or within it, full-time Christian workers or full-time professionals, but we will never realize God's vision of community until we understand what our highest calling is—and what it means to appreciate and enter into the spiritual family we were created for from the beginning.

There is no deep joy or heart-shattering tragedy that disqualifies you from the calling of Jesus on your life. You have been redeemed and restored by a Savior who accepts you and calls you to accept your spiritual brothers and sisters. He longs for you to be healed in the community he has created; and as you are healed, you, too, will participate in the healing of others.

Welcome to the messy, unpredictable, ragtag, but redeemed community of Christ. We who fully enter into this family bear witness to the prayer Jesus prayed for us almost two thousand years ago. "I have given them the glory that you gave me, that they may be one as we are one—I in them and you in me—so that they may be brought to complete unity. Then the world will know that you sent me and have loved them even as you have loved me" (John 17:22-23). May our hearts beat with the heart of Jesus. May our lives shine with the joy of our mutual calling in Christ. And may our spiritual family show Christ's love to a dying world.

Chirp, chirp went my cell phone, just as I began the writing for the highly important chapter on community you are reading right now. "Ugh. Not now. Who could that be?" I considered declining the call but saw the name of the recovery house where I minister on the caller ID. There were tears on the other end of the line, there were sobs and gasps, and there was a need, ironically, for community.

Would I have time to go down to the house to talk with her? Could I sit with her awhile? Could I take it all in, all of the fierce struggle, and give her some advice on what God wants her to do? "I went to the park and smoked a cigarette," she said. "And I asked God what in the world I am supposed to do. Your face came to my mind automatically, so I called."

It was then that I began to smile, though she could not see me. I smiled because I realized that I was just getting into the groove of my writing on community, that I really needed to apply myself to getting this chapter moving, that I needed time to work.

Yet someone in my community needed me; she needed truth, she needed my presence, she needed me to serve her. "OK," I said, "I'll be there at four."

Let's just say that after I ended the call, I felt as though God and I exchanged a wink and a smile. That day I was reminded that community matters, that she matters, and that community isn't something to be fit in when it's convenient for me to do so. Rather, community is a reality I signed up for when I came to know the Community-Giver.

❧❧❧

Tell the truth—have you ever wished you could order up community the way you order fast food? "I would like a small group made up of singles and marrieds, older and younger, with large discussions, medium prayer times, small spiritual retreats, a side of service to the broken, whipped cream and a cherry on top!" The hard truth, however, is that often we don't get to choose how and with whom we'll do community. "Christian community is not an ideal we have to realize," wrote Dietrich Bonhoeffer, "but rather a reality created by God in Christ in which we may participate."[5]

So take a deep breath. If you've accepted Christ's payment for your sins and have asked him to be King of your life, you are already a part of the big "C"—Community—Jesus came to create. The real question is: How will you participate in this community? How does one know she is doing community well? What jobs did Jesus give his restored community to do—things that they could only do together?

Read through the New Testament, and you can't help but notice how many things we should be doing for one another. Sometimes referred to as the "one anothers," there are twenty-three commands in all. And almost all of them are written by the apostle Paul. It is as if he is tripping over himself, making a great effort to remind us to be *for* one another in ways that will bring peace and joy to our relationships and honor and fame to our Creator.

The phone call that interrupted my writing reminded me of the value of simply being there for another person. I remember the hurt in her voice. I remember thinking how much courage it must have taken to call me. I remember how relieved she looked when our conversation ended that day. I must have spent twenty minutes just listening to the situation, just hearing her pain. Then I entered into it, explaining God's love for her and sharing his heart from Scripture. I asked her questions and calmed her fears, told her I believed in her. And in those tender moments, I served her—I made the conversation about her and God's plans for her, not about me. Then I prayed for her.

That simple interaction reminded me of what God's Word tells us about how to do community, of the value of "one anothering," and of the wholeness that comes when we are restored in community. Scripture makes it clear we can do for each other what I did for my friend that day:

We can share our presence.

We can share the truth.

We can share ourselves.

Now you can be present for someone, but if you're not willing to share truth and encouragement at some point, he or she might wonder why you're there at all. If you're willing to show up and to share truth, but you never bother to serve the person otherwise, you might just be labeled a hypocrite. Sure, there are many times when you will help someone only through your presence, or simply by an act of service. But eventually we need all three elements to function in healthy, life-giving community. You need the whole recipe because that's the way God designed it—it's the way he designed you.

SHARING OUR PRESENCE

When chaplains or pastors show up to comfort a patient or a family member experiencing a loss, they call the work "the ministry of presence." Ministers may not say a word to another person, but they will sit with them and be with them. They will put their arms around the hurting ones when they are unsteady, they will extend the tissue box, they will bear witness to the pain the people are experiencing.

This is a ministry each of us is called to, and it calls forth a solution to the terrible loneliness so many of us experience in the church. Acts 2, verses 42 and 46, tell us that members of the first Christian church were devoting themselves to fellowship and to breaking bread in their homes. They were doing this daily, believe it or not, and they experienced what the Greeks call *koinonia*—literally a partnership, participation, communion.

If your heart is anything like mine, it's screaming, *Yes, please!* Too often we turn our differences into deficits; we replace phone calls and face-to-face connecting with texting, Facebook, and Twitter; our families scatter far and wide, and loyalty to employers and churches and friendships often seems scarce. No wonder Jesus' vision of community sparkles so brightly and beckons so invitingly.

In this family, we are called to *accept one another* equally (Romans 15:7). No matter the political views, the hygiene standards, the intelligence level, or the ability others might have to love or benefit us in return, we accept them—we do this because our Savior has so lovingly accepted us first.

We *care for one another* (1 Corinthians 12:25) because we understand that other persons in this family will only feel the love of Jesus through a living, breathing person who is called to represent him.

And finally, we mutually *submit to one another* (Ephesians 5:21). This may be the hardest one. We've already mentioned it several times, and it has to do mostly with the way we view other people. In this important discipline, something Jesus himself modeled for us, we die to ourselves and say that we don't need to have our own way. It's a wonderfully freeing feeling to realize that "our happiness is not dependent upon getting what we want."[6]

Can you imagine what would happen if a community did these three things and did them well? You may be skeptical, realizing that sharing your presence in these ways brings new opportunities for hurt. Chances are, you've been hurt before. So when does an *ezer* stop accepting or caring for or submitting to another? She does so until it becomes destructive, until boundaries are crossed that do not promote the love that Jesus came to bring. And when she moves on, she does so to find a safe and healthy place to again explore what it means to accept, to care for, and to submit to others in the family of faith.

SHARING THE TRUTH

Has a friend ever startled you with the truth? One of my memorable truth-sharing moments came from my friend Laura, who so badly wanted me not to make a mistake in a shaky dating relationship. I remember her words clearly: "This wouldn't be worth the pain this could bring you in the end. I'd rather see you stick with Christ." Gulp. I was lonely and I longed for companionship, but dating someone who didn't fully share my faith wasn't the right solution. And Laura loved me enough to tell me straight up. Thank God for her!

In this family, we *admonish one another* gently (Colossians 3:16), sharing the truth we find in God's Word, even when it hurts. This is our job as spiritual brothers and sisters, and it's a highly important one: "Whoever turns a sinner from the error of their way will save them from death and cover over a multitude of sins" (James 5:20).

We *encourage one another*, building each other up in love (1 Thessalonians 5:11). Far too much negativity exists in the world when light and joy and truth can so easily be spread through the lips of a loving believer. Giving encouragement is free, but it reaps amazing dividends. "I admire the way you serve the poor each weekend." "I see the light of Jesus growing in you every week!" "I love the way you serve your family and friends with such tenderness and delight."

And although many of us overlook this command in Scripture, we are to *confess our sins to each other* (James 5:16) that we may be healed. Will we be forgiven if we speak only to God about our sin? God's forgiveness is available to all who truly ask in repentance. But watch what happens when you confess your struggle to a trustworthy fellow traveler—sometimes the reaction is even immediate: the sin or temptation begins to lose its hold on you. And when one person finds healing and restoration through confessing sin, a domino effect often begins to occur. Author Anne Jackson calls it the gift of going second: "When you confess . . . you're opening up this amazing opportunity for trust. You're saying, 'I'm broken.' That trust carries so much power with it. It can give people the courage to go second."[7]

SHARING OURSELVES

What's the nicest thing anyone has ever done for you? Over the years, I've become convinced that some people have the gift of giving and serving. Still, that hardly lets the rest of us off the hook!

God's Word says we are to *serve one another in love* (Galatians 5:13). This starts with the question that considers the other's needs and finds creative and life-giving ways to meet them. Maybe it is a hug, a meal in your home, or a care package for someone who's going through a trying time.

We are to *carry each other's burdens*, and so "fulfill the law of Christ" (Galatians 6:2). The load gets lighter when believers in Jesus take up or carry another's sorrow or weight. When we open ourselves up to bear another's burden or to allow someone else to help carry our own weight, the message is powerful: *you are not in this alone*.

As members of the same family, we also have the privilege of *caring for one another's physical needs* (James 2:14-19). My freshman year in college someone anonymously put money in a card to pay for a winter coat for me. I still have no idea who it was. But I needed that coat, and my spiritual family provided it. When you are blessed by God with enough to live on, you are called to give whatever you can to other members of the family who need it.

As this chapter comes to a close, I'm picturing all the members of my community strung together in a circle of relationship. I think of my friend Jim, and I am reminded what a healthy spiritual family should look like, of what is possible when one person chooses to fully enter into healing in community. I remember Katie, and I hope that God's family surrounds her even now, reminding her that she is not alone and that she is deeply loved by a God who has placed her in a spiritual family. My heart fills with gratitude for the many who have been present, who have spoken truth, and who have served me over the years.

Then, of course, I think of you—the reader—and all that your heart holds. I realize that Jesus' vision of community smacks of boldness and beauty, and it's possible it may have even taken your breath away. As you reflect on it, my prayer for you is this:

Father, we admire the oneness you display in the Trinity, and we long for it! Help your ezer *to know that her longing for community is a good gift from the Community-Giver. Remind my sister that no matter how she has been hurt in the past, you long for her to be healed and restored through fellowship in your community. Help us to accept each other as you have accepted us. And thank you, Father, for making us part of this big, beautiful family. Amen.*

Questions for Discussion

1. Do you have a friend like Jim who shows others how to do community in the church? If so, describe this person to the group.

2. How does the gospel of Jesus Christ change things for the *ezer* (the woman) and for the *adam* (the man) in community?

3. Which of the three elements of community come easiest to you? Which of them comes hardest, and why?

6

And we all, who with unveiled faces contemplate the Lord's glory, are being transformed into his image with ever-increasing glory, which comes from the Lord, who is the Spirit. (2 Corinthians 3:18)

GROWTH

THE THRIVING SISTER

"Lose pounds of belly fat," the commercial promises. "I dropped two sizes in ten days!" It's still hard not to be intrigued by some of the claims of the newest weight loss gimmicks and gadgets. When someone promises me (Jamie) I can banish my pesky postpregnancy belly, I become curious. However, there always seems to be a catch. It seems every single ad—at least the legitimate ones—come with an asterisk attached.

*With diet and exercise.

Or better yet:

*Results not typical.

As much as we would like to believe the advertisers, when it comes down to it, there's no miracle pill or gizmo that can completely take the place of good, old-fashioned hard work when it comes to weight loss. It doesn't seem fair or fun, but that's the way it is.

Sometimes I think spiritual growth is something like that. Just as I would love a magic pill or bellyband or a ten-minute Pilates video to perfect my figure, I wish there were some simple, low-commitment means of dealing with sin. "Try this magic, one-line prayer to take care of your spiritual growth, so you can get on with the rest of your life! Be a deeper, more virtuous Christian without the hassle and time commitment of devotions or church attendance!"

Sorry to burst your bubble, but that's not the way faith works either. If we are serious about growing in faith and virtue, if we want to better reflect the image of God, if we want to be real *ezers*, if we really want to live life free of sin, we're going to have to get acquainted with the spiritual disciplines.

Let me pause here and assure you that I believe wholeheartedly in the transforming power of the Holy Spirit. No spiritual growth is possible without the work of God's grace in our lives. However, by taking part in certain practices—prayer, Scripture reading, worship, and fasting, to name a few—we are opening the doors and windows of our lives to better receive God's transforming grace.[1]

WHAT ARE WE TALKING ABOUT?

One of my favorite poems is by John Donne. In his Holy Sonnet 14, he pleads for God to go to drastic measures to capture his heart.

Batter my heart, three-person'd God; for you
As yet but knock, breathe, shine, and seek to mend;
That I may rise, and stand, o'erthrow me, and bend
Your force, to break, blow, burn, and make me new.[2]

In some ways, it would be much more comfortable if God would impose his will on us in this way. However, God does not force intimacy on us and thereby violate our free will. He waits. He knocks, breathes, shines, and seeks to mend. Certainly God can break into the mundane clutter of our daily lives. We can encounter God powerfully while filing papers at work, dropping kids off at soccer practice, or scrubbing toilets. He can speak to us while we catch up with people online or mow the lawn. The Holy Spirit can reach us while we're minding our own business, but he is infinitely more likely to speak to us when we are seeking him in prayer, when we read Scripture, when we make a point of practicing the disciplines of our faith and pursue our own spiritual formation.

Some people may become uncomfortable with mention of spiritual formation. In recent years some have popularized the misconception that somehow it is tied to Eastern meditation, or that it is practiced only by Catholics. Nothing could be further from the truth. Spiritual formation is the spiritual equivalent of our emotional and physical growth over time. You will be spiritually formed whether or not you are trying to be. You will be formed toward the things of Christ or toward the world. Christian spiritual formation is simply the process of being formed in our character, internally and externally, toward Christlikeness.[3]

When we are intentionally seeking to be formed into the likeness of Christ, believers often turn to the spiritual disciplines for help. Reading Scripture, prayer, fasting, contemplation, participation in the sacraments like communion and baptism, and community—all of these are tools for the believer seeking spiritual growth.

The practice of these spiritual disciplines has been around for a long time. They were practiced by Protestant reformers in the sixteenth century who insisted that the Word of God is essential to authentic Christian spirituality. They were practiced by the early monastics who saw that a rhythm of prayer and work led to a deeper Christian experience. They were practiced by the early church as seen in Acts as they invested dramatically in their newfound church community. And they were practiced by Jesus who regularly withdrew from the crowds to seek the Father in solitude and prayer.[4]

The reality is that disciplines that were once considered a normal part of the Christian life are now considered optional practices only for the very devout. Christian spiritual formation is God's desire for all of his children. We practice the disciplines because we are disciples of Christ. As Henri Nouwen observed: "disciple" and "discipline" are the same word! Spiritual disciplines are not about control or drudgery. The disciplines serve to make space in our lives for God to act.

EVERYONE'S INVITED

I (Jamie) am an unlikely candidate to write this chapter. Some people might proudly describe themselves as "disciplined" or "hardworking." They are steady and tough and are able to school their own impulses in order to do what must be done. They are the people who expend effort toward just causes. They climb tall mountains and learn foreign languages. They master skills like martial arts or the piano or bookkeeping. They are the reason we have civilization.

I am not naturally one of these people. I would charitably describe myself as freewheeling and creative. I would rather start a good book than finish it—or better yet, I would love to just *discuss* that book. It used to be that I would say this about myself with pride. As I get older, I feel less prideful and more sheepish about these natural tendencies.

You see, when it comes to faith, the bulk of growth takes place in the mundane, muddy slog of our daily lives. Though our salvation may be decided the moment we first trust the Lord, growing in the likeness of Jesus takes time. And yes, it takes discipline.

The word "discipline" can taste unpleasant in our mouths, like sand or dry oatmeal. However, without the spiritual disciplines, we cannot hope to grow in our faith. Paul tells the Philippians to "work out your salvation with fear and trembling" (2:12). This does not sound like a pleasant process.

However, there is hope for those of you like me, for whom hard work holds very little appeal, and to-do lists never, *ever* seem to get shorter. Simply look at the very next verse. "For it is God who works in you to will and to act in order to fulfill his good purpose" (v. 13). Fortunately for us all, God has promised to do the difficult work of actually bringing about transformation; we only need to habitually surrender ourselves to him and he will do the work of spiritually forming us. This habitual surrender takes the form of the spiritual disciplines.

And the glorious thing is that since we know that God is doing the difficult job of transformation, we can trust that he will overcome our limitations in the discipline department as well. If we are willing to make space in our lives for him to work, we may be surprised that the very act of setting aside time for God becomes easier. Our attitudes and habits miraculously change over time. We were not told to be "be holy" all in our own power. God has called us to a task, and he actually plans on helping us complete it!

A DAY IN THE DISCIPLINES

When Jesus tells us to follow him, he reminds us that his yoke is easy and his burden is light. My initial reaction is, "Yes, but it's still a yoke! It's still something I'm not sure I want to cart around." I'm reminded by Dallas Willard in the *Spirit of the Disciplines* that the way of Jesus may not seem easy initially, but it is infinitely easier than a life lived under my own power. This is about more than an eternal reward: surely we can agree that an eternity in heaven is preferable to the same in hell. No, I'm learning that my daily life goes much more easily when I live it as a disciple, and not just as a believer. Let me demonstrate.

On a typical Wednesday morning, I wake up tired because of class the night before. My husband is probably on his way out the door, and my son is ready for breakfast. After feeding the baby, I allow the morning news shows to run while I fix myself breakfast and empty the dishwasher. I try to go for a short run with the jogging stroller while listening to a novel on my iPod.

I get home tired and sweaty to realize my son doesn't want to nap now—he wants to play. I try to get some writing done, but my son, the laundry, and the Internet all prove distractions, so I accomplish very little. My frustration mounts. By the time Toby is finally asleep, I just want a shower. I get myself ready for the day and tackle the kitchen, realizing I have to find time for grocery shopping at some point or else we will all go hungry soon.

The afternoon progresses much in the same way, with me feeling harried and stressed. I call my mother to tell her the latest news on her grandson and just end up griping about how he's still not sleeping through the night. My home is only half cleaned and our pantry is still empty when I stuff my son in his car seat and head off to youth group. During a discussion with my small group of teen girls, someone brings up some very serious stuff that's going on at home. I feel utterly inadequate: How am I supposed to know what scriptures to share or what to say? I try my best, but the group derails and I don't know if that individual was helped at all.

I get home late so Toby goes to bed easily, which is good because I don't have the patience for a drawn-out fight with an infant. I reward myself for making it through the day with a little television until my husband gets home. He wants to discuss how youth group went, but I just want to complain. We retreat into our own private hobbies, and I feel neglected and sullen. We go to bed, perhaps read a little, and I fall asleep thinking that the day was an utter waste.

Now let's take that same day lived as a disciple. I still wake tired and feed the baby first thing, but maybe I decide to eat breakfast with my Bible open instead of the TV on. During the run, I decide to listen to a devotional book that gets me thinking. Writing goes better because my mind has already been on task during my run, so even with a fussy baby, I get a good page down before breaking and playing with Toby until he sleeps.

I take a shower, but I then spend some time journaling before I get to the kitchen or the laundry. The time unloading the dishwasher is spent in prayer for my parents and my brother. God draws my mind to a friend who is going through a difficult time, so I pray for her and then call her when I get the chance. The conversation with my mom drifts to what God is teaching us in his Word. I don't get the house completely spotless, and I still need to go grocery shopping, but I figure out a way to get one more day of meals out of our fridge.

At youth group my earlier Scripture reading helps me speak to the troubled teen's situation. More than that, I feel led by the Holy Spirit on how to encourage her. The group gets off topic, but we're talking about important stuff and are able to end in a blessed time of prayer. At home, I am able to enjoy my husband's company and debrief after his message. We read together, and I go to sleep feeling blessed and thankful.

Which day would I rather live out again? Which yoke is easier to carry? Certainly most of my days look like a combination of the two above, and often I cannot see the benefits of a closer walk with Christ except in retrospect. Some days start with prayer and are still difficult to bear. But when I am in the Word, I live my life better. When I am praying, I am more content with myself. When I am a part of the church community, I see more joy and more grace in my life and the lives of those around me. It is far better to face each day with Christ, and the disciplines make this possible.

GETTING TO KNOW HIM

"I'm just not sure I'm exactly where God wants me to be." My dear friend was conflicted about what area of her life deserved the most attention: work, social, or church.

I felt the conflict too; I knew God was using her in all of these spheres. I didn't want to see her step back from church involvement, but I also didn't want her to discard a promising career in a field where she could be a light for Jesus.

"Well, let me ask this, have you been reading your Bible and asking God?" Upon talking to her, I learned that regular Bible study was often squeezed out by her hectic schedule. In love I challenged her, "I don't see how you can know God and know his will unless you're taking the time to be with him in the Word."

Scripture reading is essential to our spiritual formation. We have the immense privilege of being entrusted with the *very Word of God*. It is conveniently bound in two thousand plus pages, available in countless translations, and it's probably sitting on your nightstand or bookshelf right now. It is the solemn responsibility and joy of each believer to read Scripture and therein understand more about the God we serve.

As a youth pastor, my husband is an accidental collector of Jesus-themed T-shirts. Each camp, mission trip, or retreat adds another to his drawer. By far his least favorite T-shirt is one that pictures a Bible and reads, "When all else fails, read the instructions."

The Bible is not merely a set of cold instructions on how to live; it is the story of God. It is a window into the very mind of Christ. When we read the Scriptures, we are not only learning a list of things to do and things not to do but also aligning our hearts with God's heart.

But moreover, the Scripture is not something that we go to as a last resort! It should be our first stop when we are confused and discouraged by this world. Also, it must be a habitual part of our lives when we are filled with joy and peace. If we dig into the Word regularly, we find that God's hand and heart are easier to discern in our daily lives. When crisis hits, we can instantly draw on the understanding that we gain by regular study of the Bible.

Bible study does not have to follow one set pattern. Some people are helped by reading plans that design a way to read through the entire Bible in one or two years. Others prefer to read a chapter a day, one book at a time. There have been days when I spend my entire quiet time meditating on a single verse, trying to fully understand its meaning. Each of these approaches has value. Also, you may go through seasons in your personal Bible study, digesting huge swaths of Scripture one day, and slowly chewing on four potent verses the next.

Journaling is often helpful in synthesizing and applying the Scripture that we read. One useful and easy form of journaling is called the SOAP method.[5] SOAP is an acronym for Scripture, Observation, Application, and Prayer. You start by copying down a scripture that you encounter in your daily reading. Then you make basic observations about that passage—what individuals are doing in the passage or what the speaker is saying about God. The application section allows you to take these truths you've observed and apply them to your daily life. How does this understanding of God's grace impact your attitude at work or at home? In the end, write a short prayer based on these insights. A SOAP journal entry should not be more than a page in length. It's a helpful tool for making Scripture more accessible and practical.

We also encourage you to take advantage of the different translations and paraphrases that are available. If your grandmother's King James Version is hard to digest, try the New International Version or the New Living Translation. Paraphrases such as *The Message* can also be helpful, though they should not completely take the place of more literal translations.

Most importantly, don't lose heart in your pursuit of the Word. As Carla's mother used to say, you need to "plan your work and work your plan." Make use of the tools available to you, and set aside time for Scripture study. If you get off track a day or two, don't allow guilt to keep you away for days three and four. God is excited to meet with his children through the Word, no matter how long they have been away.

Aspire to be like the believers in Berea. Acts 17 says they "received the message with great eagerness and examined the Scriptures every day to see if what Paul said was true. As a result, many of them believed" (vv. 11*b*-12*a*). The Word should be approached with eagerness and consistency. As we reason out our faith by looking in the Word, we find that our faith is strengthened.

CONVERSATIONS WITH CHRIST

My grandma may be going crazy. This was the first thought that passed through my adolescent brain when I came upon my grandma muttering to herself over a sink of sudsy dishes.

"Did you need something, Grandma?"

It was a moment before she turned to me and smiled. "No, just praying."

My grandmother's faithfulness and deep love for God have made an indelible impression on me. She has long demonstrated what it means to live life as a woman of God. It would be easy to be impressed by her credentials of faith: she raised six kids on the mission field with my grandfather, she still travels around the country and the world to preach and minister to others, and she is a support and encouragement to her family and neighbors. However, I know all of these things flow out of a continual connection to God through prayer.

There are countless books on prayer. They discuss patterns of prayer, praying Scripture, prayer journals and outlines, even specific words and postures. These tools can be useful, but they can also mystify the process of learning to pray. The most important thing to remember about prayer is this: do it.

Did you catch that? When we seek a deeper prayer life, we should begin with the simple task of starting a conversation with God. In fact, if it's been a while since you've talked with God, I suggest you put this book down and take a few minutes to pray. Pray for a pressing need in your life or your family. Pray for his will revealed in your life. Pray in thanksgiving for the blessings he's given you. Pray that God would teach you how to pray.

There are no words I can put on paper that will take the place of you practicing the discipline of prayer. Yes, there are tools that can deepen our prayer lives. We should eagerly seek deeper understanding and desire to pray in a way that pleases God. However, he would rather hear from you, though your words be incorrect and unpracticed, than have you stay silent out of guilt or shame.

A relationship requires communication. If I never spoke to my husband, it would be very difficult to stay married. As *ezers*, we are geared for relationship and connection. Even the shyest or most individualistic woman can usually see the need for connection with others. Our need for communion with God goes even deeper than that. We must pursue relationship with God with the same intentionality we have for our human relationships.

Upon seeing the need for prayer, however, many believers become immediately tripped up on the logistics. How are we supposed to speak to an infinite God as flawed humans? When seeking instruction in prayer, Christians must first seek the example of Christ. The Lord's Prayer is more than lovely poetry; it is a primer on prayer for every disciple.

This, then, is how you should pray:

"Our Father in heaven,
hallowed be your name,
your kingdom come,
your will be done,
    on earth as it is in heaven.
Give us today our daily bread.
And forgive us our debts,
    as we also have forgiven our debtors.
And lead us not into temptation,
    but deliver us from the evil one."

(Matthew 6:9-13)

Fully half of this prayer is all about God, not about our needs at all. Notice that before anything else, Jesus begins with praise. Who is God? Our heavenly Father, and infinitely worthy of honor. Before anything else, we must acknowledge who God is in praise and worship.

This is immediately followed by seeking God's will. In the same way our human communications benefit from a mutual feedback and honesty, our prayer life benefits greatly when we move beyond the idea of God being a cosmic vending machine. Our prayers should not just be about our needs and wants; God must be given a chance to speak and influence our hearts as well.

Seeking God's will is not just about asking God, "What should I do with *my* life in the long-term, big picture things?" God's will is lived out in the day-to-day decisions we make. A choice to be loving toward the unlovable, a decision to share the gospel with a neighbor, resisting the urge to participate in workplace gossip: these are the daily crises that comprise God's will for our lives. The more we align ourselves daily with God's will, the more the bigger decisions will be in alignment with him as well. This is the practice of God's will done on earth as it is in heaven.

I have noticed many times we seek God's will without the intention of following it. Essentially we say, "God, tell me what your will is so I can decide whether or not I want to do it." I don't believe we can expect to hear from God when this is our attitude. Jesus' prayer for God's will did not have qualifications or room for dissenting opinion. He prayed for heaven-style obedience on earth so that we all can have the privilege of taking part in the glorious work of God's kingdom.

❧❧❧

When Jesus did move to the subject of human needs, he kept it simple. He prayed for daily bread, not a bigger house or a more cooperative roommate. I am not saying that God doesn't care about our particular frustrations and struggles. He most certainly does. And you should make a habit of praying about your troubles, be they mundane or highly specific. But when we are beginning our prayers with seeking God's will, we often find that our list of "needs" is pruned.

When I seek God's will and specifically pray in the same direction as his will, I am amazed at the results. For example, perhaps I am frustrated with the turnout of students in my Sunday school class. Initially I am tempted to pray that Gertie, Paul, and Martha would get their acts together and come back to church. However, after seeking God's will, I begin to understand that God longs for all of his children to participate in the study of his Word. I see that community can play an essential role in the revitalization of our faith. So instead I pray that God would grow the class into a strong Christlike community—that it would be a place where God's people would find encouragement and a deeper understanding of Scripture. And yes, I pray specifically for Gertie, Paul, and

Martha—that they would draw closer to Christ and know that they are welcome and loved in our community.

So when I see growth of any kind, I praise God. When a missing class member shows up, I rejoice. But the biggest difference is the immediate adjustment of my heart's perspective.

❧❧❧

The next segment of the Lord's Prayer is one that makes us uncomfortable. It requires some soul searching. We are told to pray that God would "forgive us our debts, as we also have forgiven our debtors." This requires honesty before God. We are to examine the places we have fallen short and also the times we have been disappointed or injured by others. We are then supposed to bathe all of these hurts in the grace of forgiveness. Being forgiven by God is directly linked to our willingness to forgive others. Jesus says this plainly in the next two verses: "For if you forgive other people when they sin against you, your heavenly Father will also forgive you. But if you do not forgive others their sins, your Father will not forgive your sins" (Matthew 6:14-15).

Yes, there are times when it does not feel right to forgive, but Jesus tells us to do it anyway. There are some wrongs so grievous that we cannot imagine forgiveness, but still we come before God seeking his assistance in the work of forgiveness. God can help us in this as well.

Finally Jesus prays for deliverance from temptation and evil. This shows us that we can be delivered from temptation with God's help! We don't have to resign ourselves to messing up over and over. God is again the answer to the problem of sin. He offers forgiveness when we need it and the preventative help of his Holy Spirit for each new challenge we face.

In all of this there is great freedom in prayer. Some days may be filled with praise and worship. Other days we may simply pour out our hearts about a challenge we are facing. We may be immediately burdened by the need for forgiveness, or we may be struggling with a strong temptation. These can all be facets of a vibrant prayer life. Ultimately we must see prayer as more than a forum for requesting miracles. It is an honest conversation of the heart.

DOING THE WORK

I was sitting in a chapel service my senior year of college, trying to discreetly study for an impending exam, when I heard the speaker say something I had never heard before in all my years of church.

"If you're not feeling the Holy Spirit, and you're tired of singing in worship, and if you feel like your prayers are bouncing off the ceiling, *keep doing it anyway*."

What? I thought. *Surely he can't mean I should fake religion?* But he continued in the same vein. "Keep raising your hands in worship; keep going to church; keep reading your Bible. Because you never know when God's going to break through. And the more you do the work, the more opportunities you're giving the Holy Spirit to wake you up and change your heart."

I have wrestled with what he said, and I have prayed over it. And in practice I feel I have to agree that it's true. We are holistic beings: the mind, the soul, and the body are not separate entities but all interconnected pieces of the same whole. Though many adolescents may roll their eyes when their parents advise that they "put on a happy face," it remains good advice. Often our hearts and minds follow where our bodies lead.

Jesus ministered with a holistic understanding of humankind. He not only forgave sins but also healed the lame. He was concerned about the entirety of the human experience, not just their eternal destination. In Mark 5, when he encountered the woman with a bleeding disorder, Jesus not only impacted her physically but restored her socially as well. Her disorder would have isolated her as unclean from her community, but Jesus did away with that barrier. He also affirmed her faith and told her to go in peace. He understood that our physical state impacts our emotional and spiritual state and vice versa.

❧❧❧

When I was in high school, we lived in West Africa and attended a small Senegalese church. One worship chorus we sang often was "Plus Haut." This means "Higher" in French. The congregation would jump up and down and wave their hands in the air as they sang, "higher, higher! Jesus is higher!" Then they would stomp and grind their feet into the ground as they sang about Satan being lower and trampled underfoot. The uninhibited expression of praise and victory over Satan was electrifying. As we stomped our feet we began to feel truly set free from the snares of the devil.

Still now, in a more reserved North American congregation, when I raise my hands in worship, I find that my heart is raised as well. When I actually get on my knees or go down to the church altar to pray, I have a better sense of entering God's presence. If we are faithful to do the work of faith, even when we aren't feeling spiritual, we eventually find that our hearts have been changed in the process.

More than this, however, there is reciprocal movement on God's part. When we draw near to God, we are promised that he will draw near to us (James 4:8). Perhaps we will find that God has been near us all along, and we simply have not taken the time to see him.

❧❧❧

The disciplines are our way of faithfully turning toward God and focusing on him. There are more disciplines that deserve mention than Bible study and prayer. Participation in sacraments like communion and baptism is essential; after all, these are practices that were given to us directly by Jesus as a means of grace in our lives! The simple act of investing in a church community by regular attendance can grow our faith through connection to fellow believers. Our souls can find new spiritual sustenance when we practice the discipline of fasting.

Study, meditation, simplicity, and service—there are so many ways for us to seek God through the disciplines. I encourage you to look for new ways to practice your faith, taking advantage of the many resources that are available today.[6] The disciplines are an opportunity for us to respond to God's grace. They are not a chore, but a privilege. We have tools that are useful for growing in our faith; it's time we picked them up and learned how to use them.

THE SECRET OF TRANSFORMATION

I have some bad news. You can pick up the tools and learn to use them like an expert, and it will not make a real difference in your soul. You can try very, very hard—give it everything you have—and you will never get rid of sin or grow in virtue. You cannot will or work yourself into spiritual growth.

You see, *we are still helpless.* We are still frail humans. The source of transformation is found not in ourselves but in our Savior!

Spiritual formation is not something we do, but it is something God does in us. As we pursue the disciplines, we must always be wary of our tendency to do good deeds in our own strength. If you feel crushing guilt after missing a day of devotions, might you secretly be thinking your spiritual growth is all up to you? If you feel depressed and discouraged when you slide into temptation again, is it because you think that you can do it all on your own? These are signs you're living as a moralist. You're missing the essential element of grace!

Let me reassert: transformation is possible. However, it's not going to happen simply because we are faithful or hardworking enough. It happens when God through the Holy Spirit does the work in our hearts. Our job is merely to open windows and unlock doors—to give the Spirit free access to our lives.

When we trip over our fallenness, it should not be an opportunity for guilt, but rather a blessed excuse to throw our arms wide and run back to the Father. God is the source: he is strong where we are weak and faithful where we are distracted.

The one who runs to the Father in her weakness is the same one who experiences victory. By making a habit of turning to God, we give him opportunity to transform us. It may not always happen overnight, but it does happen.

Many times I have prayed fervently about a sin, habitually turning it over to God. Months later, I realize I am not struggling with it the same way I used to. There is a gorgeous optimism to the belief that we can be made holy through the work of the Holy Spirit. In Romans 8, Paul talks of being "set . . . free from the law of sin and death" (v. 2). That freedom is a function of Jesus' work of redemption and the gift of the Holy Spirit. We find that freedom by steady spiritual growth, by allowing the Holy Spirit to heal us as we discussed earlier, and by a daily practice of spiritual formation.

The gift of the Spirit is the source and navigator of our spiritual formation. Yes, we must seek earnestly to practice the disciplines. For as we chase after the things of God, the Holy Spirit will make us new.

Questions for Discussion

1. In this chapter, Jamie discusses the difference spiritual disciplines make in the course of a normal day. How does a day of your life look different with or without the practice of the disciplines?

2. What were you doing the last time you experienced the presence of God? What role did prayer and Scripture play?

3. In the Lord's Prayer, Jesus placed great importance on forgiveness. When in your life have you been tempted to hold on to hurt or anger? How would forgiveness change that situation?

So Christ himself gave the apostles, the prophets, the evangelists, the pastors and teachers, to equip his people for works of service, so that the body of Christ may be built up. (Ephesians 4:11-12)

7

RESTORED

THE SERVING WOMAN

At first glance, the life of Therese Martin was not exceptional. The youngest of five girls, she did not come from a fashionable or influential family. She decided at a young age to become a nun, just like her sisters. She wrote a few inexpert journals at her sister's prodding, and then succumbed to illness and died at the tender age of twenty-four.

It seems strange then that her autobiography has sold millions of copies. It's fascinating that her ideas have caught the imagination and attention of so many Christians. Aside from a pilgrimage to Rome when she was fifteen, she never left her home country of France, yet she is now the patron saint of missionaries.

Therese said that God gave her a great "thirst for souls." She longed to see people brought to repentance in Christ. She resolved, however, that the way she could best serve God was through living as a "little soul" as compared with the greatness of God. Her sole purpose was "to love Jesus unto folly." She prayed diligently for the lost and worked tirelessly to love and serve all with whom she came in contact. Therese's humble existence has deeply impacted countless people. Truly God has granted her the harvest that she longed to see.

It seems mysterious and wonderful that God's greatness should shine so brightly through a woman whose chief concern was that she should "remain *little* and become this more and more."[1] She is a demonstration of the fact that effective service in the kingdom of God has nothing to do with greatness or worthiness. It is not dependent upon talent or vocation. It begins when we are willing to take on the attitude of a servant and allow love to infiltrate all areas of our life.

FOLLOW THE LEADER

The apostle Peter had some serious shortcomings, and I like to think he was aware of the fact. He knew he was just a fisherman; he knew he wasn't the most educated guy. He had faith, but it wasn't quite enough for walking on water. He had insights, but they were only occasional. One day Jesus was calling Peter a stone on which he would build his church and the next he rebuked him sharply. Peter didn't always have his act together.

But he knew who Jesus was. The Spirit had revealed the Messiah to him, and he had some inkling of the adventure he was caught up in. He had even witnessed Jesus' transfiguration, God's glory on the mountaintop.

So when Jesus—the teacher, the Messiah—tucked a towel around his waist and knelt down to wash Peter's feet, it's no wonder Peter objected! How could the Messiah crouch at a fallible fisherman's feet and do the work of a servant?

❧❧❧

Our servant Savior is still a challenge to his disciples. Jesus, our example, never insisted on his rights. He did not dominate those who followed him. Instead, he knelt to wash feet, and more than that, he died for our salvation!

Jesus went beyond simply setting the example of service; he extended the call to those who followed him. After his resurrection, Jesus had a conversation with Peter:

> When they had finished eating, Jesus said to Simon Peter, "Simon son of John, do you love me more than these?"
>
> "Yes, Lord," he said, "you know that I love you."
>
> Jesus said, "Feed my lambs."
>
> Again Jesus said, "Simon son of John, do you love me?"
>
> He answered, "Yes, Lord, you know that I love you."

Jesus said, "Take care of my sheep."

(John 21:15-16)

Jesus teaches us that the greatest commandment is to love God (Matthew 22:37-38). But Jesus asked Peter to demonstrate his love by serving Jesus' flock. One of the greatest ways we can demonstrate our love for Jesus is by rolling up our sleeves and joining him in his work.

Service is still at the core of what it is to be a Christian. And yes, it is at the very core of what it is to be an *ezer*—growing and thriving in the image of God.

When we look at the creation story we see that Eve was not taking a backseat in the activity. In earlier chapters we've mentioned that she was designed to share in the work, to rescue from solitude, to join in the very dance of the Trinity. Eve was a part of the blessing to be fruitful, to rule and subdue the earth. Even the word *ezer* seems inextricable from activity and service. We are designed to be a strong helping power, to be an agent of rescue for others. Just as God showed himself to be a God of action in the garden of Eden, he created us to get in on his work.

THE CALL OF EVERY BELIEVER

Heather was frustrated with her life. Her beautiful plans to go to college full time and make a difference in the world seemed thwarted by her continual health problems. She wanted to get on with her life but felt stuck and ineffectual. Heather prayed, "God, if you're going to take school from me, you're going to have to give me something else—some other way to serve."

Just a few days later, she was invited to lead a small group of teen girls once a week. She wasn't sure she could handle the time commitment, but she decided to try it anyway.

It's been three years since Heather made that decision, and I can honestly say I've rarely seen someone serve so joyfully in the church! She delights in the time she gets to spend with "her girls." When she can't be present in person, she reaches out to them via Facebook and phone. God has equipped her to serve and given her great joy in doing so!

Serving in the church is not a matter of drudgery or obligation. There is real pleasure in being about the business of Jesus. It is a natural response to the outpouring of God's grace in our lives. If God has shown you your worth, if he has demonstrated the blessed healing that is found in community, if he is working in your life to form you into his image, then what could be more suitable than service in his kingdom?

In Paul's letter to the church in Ephesus, he goes to great lengths to make sure his readers understand that we are reconciled to God by grace through faith. God is the One who does the work of reconciliation, and it is our faith that counts, not our effort. However, he concludes, "For we are God's handiwork, *created in Christ Jesus to do good works*, which God prepared in advance for us to do" (Ephesians 2:10, emphasis added). When we serve in the kingdom, we are fulfilling the purpose for which we were created and redeemed! What could be more joyful and right than that?

James more firmly states, "As the body without the spirit is dead, so faith without deeds is dead" (2:26). Service puts action to our faith. It takes the grace that starts in our hearts and minds and pushes it out to our hands and feet, which can then get busy making a difference in the world.

Like Heather, you probably could find good reasons to not be involved. Health problems, busy schedules, or lingering feelings of inadequacy can make service seem inconvenient if not impossible. However, the truth is that we glorify God only when we serve in love through the power of the Holy Spirit. You feel like you don't have what it takes to serve? Good! Only when we depend on God will we truly experience joy in the kingdom work that we do.

SPIRITUAL GIFTS

We've talked a lot about "service" and "good works," but what does that mean? What qualifies as kingdom work?

Paul's epistles contain a lot of talk about spiritual gifts, particularly three main lists found in Romans 12, 1 Corinthians 12, and Ephesians 4. These have given birth to countless spiritual gift inventories and checklists. It is tempting to scour these passages and consider, "Do I have the gift of teaching? Or possibly discernment? What does Paul mean by prophecy, or exhortation?" It can be baffling to try and place ourselves in the proper category, and what do we do if none of these designated spots seems to fit?

Well, there is overlap but also a lot of variety in Paul's lists. No two are exactly alike. Reading all of these passages back to back, one can see that no list is exhaustive. Rather, Scripture shows there are many ways to serve the kingdom. God gifts each individual in distinct ways.

There are some common elements, however. First, all Christian service—no matter what your gifting—is a work of God's grace in our lives. Real kingdom work is done out of the power and presence of the Holy Spirit.

> There are different kinds of gifts, but the same Spirit distributes them. There are different kinds of service, but the same Lord. There are different kinds of working, but in all of them and in everyone it is the same God at work. (1 Corinthians 12:4-6)

Though service is in many ways an expression of our uniqueness, each gift is already an example of God's good work in our lives. The very talents and skills we use are gifts from the Lord. We don't serve under our own power.

Similarly, anything we do in service to God will necessarily be in alignment with his will as it is already known in Scripture. Service for the kingdom does not include gossip or hurling angry insults or drunkenness. I've known girls who attempt "missionary dating" unbelievers, only to fall into sinful habits themselves. When first considering "Can this be a service to the kingdom?" ask yourself if it lines up with Scripture.

Second, the work we do is focused on the goal of building up the body of Christ. No spiritual gift exists in a vacuum—when we work in the Spirit, our efforts bring about good for the body of Christ. This could mean building up your local church through teaching Sunday school or encouraging and supporting pastors. It could include cooking meals for someone who just had a baby or working with a praise band to ensure musical excellence in an Easter program. It will not be self-serving. It cannot be just about you and God. Service connects us to the rest of the church.

Third, no work can be kingdom work unless it is bathed in love. It is no accident that in 1 Corinthians 13 Paul interrupts his treatise on spiritual gifts with the most well-known discussion of love in the Bible. Though it is a pretty part of many marriage ceremonies, what Paul is really trying to communicate is tough and dramatic. Nothing we say is more than a loud noise without love. Nothing we do is more than twiddling our thumbs without love. We know nothing, and we have nothing without love. The picture painted in 1 Corinthians 13 is nothing less than a picture of our Savior Jesus.

So service is a work of the Holy Spirit in our lives; it builds up the body of Christ, and it is full of love. If these conditions are met by your activity, congratulations! You're already involved in Christian service, whether or not you knew it. It may be unusual service. A friend of mine insists that her mother has the spiritual gift of shopping! I was skeptical at first, but as I've seen this woman use her bargain hunting skills to bless others, I've become convinced she's right. God can use you to sing solos, play with toddlers, repair toilets, or lead discussions. We serve an enormously creative God.

UNEASY OBEDIENCE

When I was a little girl, my favorite book of the Bible was probably Esther. I was raised on the mission field, and Sunday services were often in languages I didn't understand, but I had my Bible with me and I could usually finish the story of Esther before the sermon was over. It had adventure, intrigue, a beautiful heroine, and a happy ending. Esther's story caught my imagination and still holds it to this day.

As I've aged, though, I've noticed how little of Esther's life was under her control. She was among the Jews in exile, and her parents were dead. She was taken from her cousin and placed in a harem, further displaced and objectified.

Esther found herself queen of a godless nation, forced to hide her faith and ethnicity. And yet, at just the right time, God used her mightily. Esther's service to God was responding to the urgent need that was placed in front of her. In a time of crisis, Esther faced her fear and used the gifts and position she was granted to rescue her people.

Sometimes God places us in an ideal position to serve. He ordains the time and place, gifts us for the work, and clearly reveals the opportunity. And yet, in those instances, service can *still* be uncomfortable, even downright frightening. Yes, service in the kingdom brings peace and joy, but it may not be easy.

I have found this to be true in my own life. When I was only a year out of college, my husband and I moved to Fort Wayne so he could take up full-time youth ministry at Grace Point Church, where we still serve. I quickly decided to settle into our church's choir. I love music and had found fulfillment in music ministry at our former church. During that first summer, however, the choir wasn't meeting regularly, so I bided my time with the youth group on Wednesday nights when choir would ordinarily meet.

By the time choir started up again in the fall, I found my heart greatly burdened for the youth, even though that was far out of my comfort zone. Youth ministry was my husband's calling, not mine! After a great deal of prayer and frustration, I decided to continue spending my Wednesdays with the youth.

Not long after that, God opened doors for me to begin teaching a new young adult Sunday school class—another ministry that would not have been possible if I were still involved in music ministry. It was also another job for which I initially felt very unqualified.

However, the act of being obedient changed my heart. As I spent more time around teens and as I planned Sunday school lessons, I learned that God knew what he was doing when he called me. In fact, he knew much better than I did.

FOLLOW YOUR ANGUISH

Finding a ministry home can sometimes be a long process. And we may find that we are not as "settled" as we imagine we are. A willing servant often finds her ministry evolves as she grows and learns. This can mean a clear change in focus like I experienced, but it can also mean a change of venue, means, or scale.

One can go from directing a musical to leading a worship band. A Bible study that starts in your kitchen can spread to envelop your entire neighborhood and your city. Gifts used faithfully in your home church can have an impact in congregations across the globe.

It is sometimes difficult, however, to start in service because there are so many worthy causes. So much need presents itself daily, and one cannot possibly address every single need. Effective service begins with allowing God to give us his heart for our own. It begins when our hearts start to break over the things that break our Father's heart.

As Americans, I know we take little delight in truly dwelling on the things that grieve the heart of God, such as injustice, poverty, and pain. We furrow our brows and suck our teeth and exclaim that it is a real shame and someone should do something. We are temporarily more grateful for our blessings and our safety. We move on with our daily lives.

Instead, though, a servant heart willingly sits in that anguish for a time. When Nehemiah learned about the ruin of Jerusalem's wall and the difficulties faced by the remnant, he did not simply go back to his cushy job; he mourned, fasted, and prayed for days. He allowed that sorrow to infiltrate his heart so that he was moved to act on it.[2]

When trying to determine where to serve, the best place to start is our anguish. Perhaps you see a deep need for biblical literacy and should consider ways you can teach believers about Scripture. Maybe your mind goes immediately to those who are lost, and you need to find opportunities to share the gift of salvation. You could feel particularly burdened for at-risk children or those who struggle to feed their families. I think of how Carla's heart has been heavily burdened by the continuing horrors of gender-based violence around the world. Certainly all of the women serving to fight this problem feel a deep, sorrowful desire to see women understand their value to God.

When we embrace our anguish, we will find ourselves moved to action in dynamic and unexpected ways. Rather than being afraid of anguish, we must open ourselves up to it, face it, and let it change us.[3]

Often we find that God has particularly equipped us to answer the need that weighs on our hearts. Another way to discern where to serve is simply to see where God is already at work in your life. Sometimes by reflecting on those times when we truly knew that we were used by God, we can see new opportunities to do more of the same.

MIXED SIGNALS

I was reading through 1 Corinthians to dig into Paul's teachings about spiritual gifts. Chapter 12: many gifts but one Spirit—awesome! Chapter 13: your gifts are useless without love—beautiful! And chapter 14: women should remain silent in church. I let out a groan of frustration. I wanted to throw my Bible across the room. (I didn't, but I did close it for the day.)

This passage and a few others still perplex and trip up many believers, myself included. Why does Paul say women must be silent when a few chapters earlier he's taking it as granted that they will be prophesying and praying in church? Is this the same Paul who greeted so many women as personal friends and fellow ministers in Romans 16? The same man who reiterates that there is now no Jew nor Greek, slave nor free, male nor female, but we are all heirs of God's promise? (Galatians 3:26-29).

Unlike my two sisters I am writing with, I have not experienced a call into formal ministry. However, I still struggle with the implication that somehow women aren't fit for all types of kingdom service. What does this mean for women who are gifted to lead and teach? What about those who find themselves in church leadership by default? What does this mean for me?

❧❧❧

So I continued to read, and I brought my difficult questions to those I respected—including my husband, as Paul suggests in this passage! This was a peace-granting exercise. In the end, I felt strongly that Paul did not intend to write a blanket prescription for all circumstances but was instead trying to curtail a specific problem. Undereducated women were interrupting the service with questions that held the whole congregation back. This was practically disruptive, but also offended the cultural sensibilities of the time.[4]

I approached all the passages that I found troubling in a similar way. Whereas in the past I had shrugged uncomfortably and moved on to the next chapter, I now stared my concerns in the face. I tried to gain a better understanding of specific cultural context as well as the story of redemption that is traced through all of Scripture. I read many books and commentaries and heard personal testimonies; I took advantage of the many resources that addressed my questions thoroughly. I would encourage women to seek out the truth of these passages for themselves!

Two things quickly became evident to me. First, biblical interpretation is tricky—that's one of the reasons there are so many different perspectives on tough issues. The difficulty shouldn't inspire anger, however, and the answer isn't to give up on the questions or on Scripture!

Second, the entirety of Scripture rings with the truth that God values his children, both male and female. Jesus' ministry both in life and death serves to counteract the curse of sin and its many consequences, and also to aid all believers in reestablishing intimacy with God.

The evidence of that intimacy is found in service to God and to others. As God's "strong helpers," women are immediately defined as agents of action. Women help, they rescue others from solitude, they are strong and powerful. This is not a picture of a being created to sit quietly by, watching others share, grow, and serve.

So women, as God has equipped you, serve!

But maybe you feel like there are certain doors to service that are closed to you in your church because of gender or other factors.

My husband looked at me like I was crazy when I brought up this subject. "The church always needs volunteers!" There are classes that need to be taught, food pantries that need to be filled, kids that need to be mentored, and visitors that need to be greeted. The average church never has enough help.

Even if certain doors are closed, others are open. Service is not only teaching from the pulpit but also filling someone's chipped mug with coffee in a church basement while talking with them about their illness. Service can be driving a bus full of kids to laser tag or photocopying music in the church office. Service is singing in the choir or praying with a friend at the altar.

Obedience in the small, unglamorous things is where God begins to form us. You may feel an affinity for preaching and leadership, but if you are not willing to do the small things first and always, you will not be the leader God has called you to be. I think of a woman who pastors a church with her husband. I remember her relating the time she had to clean vomit off the floor of the church foyer because there was no one else willing to do it. She felt frustrated and undignified, but she did it, and God blessed her in that endeavor.

This is the paradox of leadership as Jesus demonstrated it. If you want to become first, you must become last. To lead, you must be the first to serve.

Our friend Peter must have felt rather bruised when Jesus asked him a third time, "Simon son of John, do you love me?" Peter replied:

"Lord, you know all things; you know that I love you."

> Jesus said, "Feed my sheep. Very truly I tell you, when you were younger you dressed yourself and went where you wanted; but when you are old you will stretch out your hands, and someone else will dress you and lead you where you do not want to go." Jesus said this to indicate the kind of death by which Peter would glorify God. Then he said to him, "Follow me!" (John 21:17-19)

Peter was called to a dramatic life of giving up his own wants and plans and following Jesus by loving and serving. That sort of sacrifice is still an essential part of service and leadership today.

A time may come when a woman who feels called into leadership must make hard decisions. That could include a loving challenge to the conventions held by your church. It could mean seeking a congregation that will support your calling. However, the answer is never nurturing bitterness or self-glorification. Jesus' example of love and humility must be our model at all turns, or else our ministry will be for nothing.

NOT NOW, BUT SOMEDAY . . .

So often I feel women in the church are waiting for a neon sign in the sky to begin in service. We too easily put off big convictions and callings because we feel unprepared or unequipped—they go into the "someday" part of our brain. "Someday I will begin to minister to children—when I get a little more experience." "Someday I will give money to that charity—when I get a raise." "I will disciple that new believer—once I know the Bible a little better."

We must be faithful to move in the direction of that "someday." So you can't preach on Sunday mornings right now because of your church's policy or your lack of training. Read to educate yourself. Look for opportunities to share God's truth in other venues: Sunday school, exhorting a friend, answering a coworker's questions.

Jesus taught that we must be faithful with these small things first. In Matthew 25:14-30, he tells us the parable of the talents. Three servants are given money to safeguard while their master is away. Two put the money to work and double the funds. The master returns to say, "Well done, good and faithful servant! You have been faithful with a few things; I will put you in charge of many things. Come and share your master's happiness!" (v. 21).

The final servant, however, buries the gift given by the master. Out of fear, the third servant digs a hole and forgets about the talent. The master's response is harsh:

> "You wicked, lazy servant! So you knew that I harvest where I have not sown and gather where I have not scattered seed? Well then, you should have put my money on deposit with the bankers, so that when I returned I would have received it back with interest.
>
> "So take the bag of gold from him and give it to the one who has ten bags. For whoever has will be given more, and they will have an abundance. Whoever does not have, even

what they have will be taken from them. And throw that worthless servant outside, into the darkness, where there will be weeping and gnashing of teeth." (Vv. 26-30)

When we sense a call to service but refuse to answer, it is no small matter. God takes it very seriously. God is not afraid you will mess up his plans. He isn't looking for qualified applicants with a certain amount of experience. The only way we can disappoint him is if we sit on our hands and do nothing.

At the same time, know that it is never too late to join in. The value God has given you cannot be stolen or diminished by life's circumstances. There is still room for you to serve, still time to use the talents God has entrusted to you.

HOW *NOT* TO SERVE

"I remember the small church we attended when we were first married. We did *everything* there." Our Sunday school conversation had turned to the topic of service, and one busy woman was sharing her story. "We were doing a lot of good stuff, but I never saw my husband, and I hardly slept at night. We eventually had to just say, '*Enough*!'"

I knew this woman to still be active in ministry. No one could accuse her of burying talents. However, she had come dangerously close to burnout and had to learn the hard way to set boundaries.

The church, unfortunately, is not immune to "the law of the vital few." Alternately known as the "Pareto Principle" or the "80/20 Rule," the core concept is the same. A few individuals will find themselves doing the bulk of the necessary work. In businesses, this shows up when 20 percent of the clients produce 80 percent of the sales profits, or when 20 percent of the employees do 80 percent of the work. In the church, a valiant few believers take on the larger part of the work that needs to be done. One or two families keep countless ministries afloat by themselves while the majority of the congregation acts as spectators.[5]

For those of you who suspect you may be part of the overworked 20 percent, it may be time to take a deep breath and a step back. It is easy to feel guilty or obligated when you are presented with a new opportunity to serve. And it's tempting for pastors to keep calling the same overinvolved people over and over again. The reason is simple: they can be counted on to say yes!

But when I advocate service in the church, I am not advocating burnout. Know your own limits and respect them. It's okay to say no sometimes, and learning the skill of maintaining boundaries will enable you to keep serving for a much longer time. If God is laying something on your heart and you feel you need to say yes to a new ministry, examine your other commitments. Is there another area where you need to step back and allow someone else to get involved?

What a blessing it is to realize our own limitations. When we step back, we often see God raise up others to meet needs that we could not meet on our own.

I met an individual once who worked a full-time job, ran her church's youth program, led the praise team, sat on the church board, and ran a boys and girls club outside of church. I commented, "Well, you must get tired!" Her response was a grin as she said, "This is just what I do."

I left that conversation unsettled. I couldn't shake the impression of pride that eked out of her reply. She had become so used to doing everything in the church that she had forgotten that she wasn't the one keeping it running in the first place! (Hint: it's God.)

Perhaps many who find themselves overextended in ministry secretly believe that they are the ones running the show. "I can't possibly stop doing X! What would they do without me?" In reality, ministries that are God-focused and God-directed can handle a change in leadership. More than that, sometimes a transition can breathe new life into a program that has gone stale. In other cases, it may be appropriate to let certain ministries stop for a time so that the need can be realized and met by someone new.

Obviously these are decisions that must be made with prayer. But whatever the circumstance, God is the source and the director of our service. He is the One we serve and the means by which we serve. Truly none of it is possible without him.

WHATEVER YOU DO . . .

Service by the direction of and through the power of the Holy Spirit is a glorious thing. At times, though, it is difficult to focus on the Spirit, or even to believe that service is possible, when faced with the daily grind of a to-do list. Noisy coworkers and stubborn children discourage us. Illness and tragedy waylay us. There just aren't enough hours in the day to spend even one doing "church stuff."

An *ezer* may be designed for action, but all your energy is used up at the end of the day. You simply aren't up to the challenge.

Good. God tells us that's a perfectly okay place to start. "And whatever you do, whether in word or deed, do it all in the name of the Lord Jesus, giving thanks to God the Father through him" (Colossians 3:17). In Colossians 3, Paul mentions many ways to glorify God, but in the end he encourages believers simply to make Jesus the motivation behind every little thing they do. In your daily life—the errands, chores, and obligations—everything can be an act of service to our King Jesus.

Brother Lawrence, a seventeenth-century monk, was very familiar with kitchen work. He made a practice of doing every task, large or small, as an act of devotion to God. He said, "It is not necessary to have great things to do. I turn my little omelet in the pan for the love of God; and when it is finished . . . adore my God who gave me the grace to make it."[6] He wrote that even the mundane and distasteful tasks of life are "the Lord's work."

Saint Therese of Lisieux would have said we are to "make love our vocation."[7] Any small task done with love can be glorious service to God and to others. A tired postal worker, a hungry baby, a busy coworker: all these can be greatly blessed by small, everyday actions suffused with God's love.

An *ezer* who is truly restored to the image of God—who understands her worth and is living out of the power of the Spirit—will not always be busy. She may not be important in the world's eyes. She has bad hair days. Her to-do lists aren't any shorter than the next woman's. But she lets God's love shine through her smallest actions. Ultimately, this is how she serves God and builds up fellow believers.

Questions for Discussion

1. Service can take many different forms. What are some of the opportunities you've had to serve others today?

2. Do you feel like you are part of the 80 percent or the 20 percent in your local church? If you're taking more of a backseat, why do you think that is? If you're very involved, how are your commitments blessing or stressing you?

3. Is there a particular need or injustice over which you feel anguish? How might God be calling you to intervene? What are some small, practical ways in which God can use you to address the need this week?

EPILOGUE

❧ The writing of this work has been a spiritual journey for Suzanne, Jamie, and me. The project has taken us more than three years to complete, and this final form has morphed from the original project because of all that we have learned along the way. I am grateful for my sister *ezers* who have embodied the sisterhood throughout this project. We have laughed, cried, and labored together to bring this work to our sisters in Christ.

It seems that for far too long God's *ezers* have been like the light that has been hidden. In Matthew 5:15 Jesus said, "Neither do people light a lamp and put it under a bowl. Instead they put it on its stand, and it gives light to everyone in the house." We as women are God's light and we are to be set free to shine the message of hope and freedom into the world.

Our prayer is that you have traveled this journey with us; from uncovering the *ezer*, to discovering the *blessed alliance*, to encountering the *sisterhood*, discovering wholeness and then being set free to live out your life in community, growing in spiritual formation and then finally your place of service in the kingdom. We are God's daughters who are at peace, relaxing in him, growing in Christlikeness, and becoming a powerful reflection of Jesus to our world. Thanks for joining us. We hope to see you along the way.

NOTES

INTRODUCTION

1. Lilian Calles Barger, *Eve's Revenge: Women and a Spirituality of the Body* (Grand Rapids, Mich.: Brazos Press, 2003), 14, 22.

2. Susan J. Douglas, *Enlightened Sexism: The Seductive Message That Feminism's Work Is Done* (New York: Times Books, 2010), 9.

3. Augustine, *On the Trinity* 12.7, in *Fathers of the Church*, vol. 45, trans. Stephen McKenna (Washington, DC: Catholic University of America Publications, 1963).

"The woman together with her husband is the image of God, so that the whole substance is one image. But when she is assigned as a helpmate, a function that pertains to her alone, then she is not the image of God, but as far as the man is concerned, he is by himself alone the image of God, just as fully and completely as when he and the woman are joined together into one."

CHAPTER 1

1. Tertullian, *On the Apparel of Women* in *Ante-Nicene Fathers*, vol. 4, book 1, chap. 1.

2. Thomas Aquinas, *Summa Theologiae*. See also Marie I. George, *What Aquinas Really Said About Women* in *First Things*, December 1999, accessed December 27, 2012, http://www.firstthings.com/article/2007/01/what-aquinas-really-said-about-women-24.

3. Scot McKnight, *The Blue Parakeet: Rethinking How You Read the Bible* (Grand Rapids, Mich.: Zondervan, 2008), 166.

4. James Montgomery Boice, *Genesis: An Expositional Commentary* (Grand Rapids, Mich.: Baker Books, 1998), 25.

5. Carolyn Custis James, *Half the Church: Recapturing God's Global Vision for Women* (Grand Rapids, Mich.: Zondervan, 2010), 51.

6. Sir Edward Tias Cook, *The Life of Florence Nightingale*, vol. 1 (London: Macmillan and Co. Ltd., 1914), 57.

7. Catherine Clark Kroeger and Mary J. Evans, *The IVP Women's Bible Commentary* (Downers Grove, Ill.: InterVarsity Press, 2002), 2-3.

8. Allen P. Ross, *Creation and Blessing: A Guide to the Study and Exposition of Genesis* (Grand Rapids, Mich.: Baker Books, 1996), 112-13.

9. Boice, *Genesis*, 88.

10. God as *ezer*: see Exodus 18:4; Deuteronomy 33:7, 26, 29; Psalms 20:2; 33:20; 70:5; 89:19; 115:9, 10, 11; 121:1, 2; 124:8; 146:5; and Hosea 13:9.

11. Interview with Dr. Sarah Coleson Derck, assistant professor of Old Testament, Houghton College, June 14, 2011.

12. Adapted from Joseph E. Coleson, "Ezer Cenegdo: A Power Like Him, Facing Him as Equal," accessed June 28, 2011, www.whwomenclergy.org, www.whwomenclergy.org/booklets/power_like_him.php.

13. Carolyn Custis James, *When Life and Beliefs Collide: How Knowing God Makes a Difference* (Grand Rapids, Mich.: Zondervan, 2010), 184-85.

CHAPTER 2

1. This phrase was first coined by Carolyn Custis James in *Lost Women of the Bible: Finding Strength and Significance through Their Stories.* (Grand Rapids, Mich.: Zondervan, 2005), 37.

2. Kent Brower, "The Trinity" (lecture, Nazarene Theological Seminary, Kansas City, 2003).

3. Eve's reputation has been tarnished through the centuries as many authors clearly placed the blame of sin squarely on her shoulders and then went on to place an Eve in every female. Mary Magdalene's reputation was severely tarnished in the sixth century when Pope Leo, in one of his homilies, portrayed her as a prostitute (an assertion which cannot be found within Scripture).

4. Quoted in Phoebe Palmer, *Promise of the Father* (New York: W. C. Palmer, Jr., 1872), 52.

5. Alan F. Johnson, *How I Changed My Mind about Women in Leadership: Compelling Stories from Prominent Evangelicals* (Grand Rapids, Mich.: Zondervan, 2010), Kindle edition, 115-16.

6. Jim Henderson, George Barna, and Lynne Hybels, *The Resignation of Eve* (Carol Stream, Ill.: Tyndale House Publishers, 2012), Kindle edition, 108.

7. Johnson, *Women in Leadership*, 44.

CHAPTER 3

1. Euclid, *Euclid's Elements*, accessed December 13, 2012, http://www.themathpage.com/aBookI/propI-2-3.htm.

2. Rachel Held Evans, A *Year of Biblical Womanhood: How a Liberated Woman Found Herself Sitting on Her Roof, Covering Her Head, and Calling Her Husband "Master"* (Nashville: Thomas Nelson, 2012), Kindle edition, xvii.

3. Nicole Williams, "Infographic: Women and Mentoring in the United States," LinkedIn Blog, accessed December 13, 2012, http://blog.linkedin.com/2011/10/25/mentoring-women/.

4. Matthew Towles, "How Men Benefit from Having Female Mentors," *The Atlantic*, accessed December 13, 2012, http://www.theatlantic.com/sexes/archive/2012/11/how-men-benefit-from-having-female-mentors/265523/.

CHAPTER 4

1. Mr. Ron McClellan went on to become a lifelong friend and a music professor at MidAmerica Nazarene University. During my years as a missionary he brought his Jazz Band to the mission field where we were able to collaborate in ministry. His presence there that day was a gift from God.

2. Jonnie Jernigan, "Redeemed Through the Blood" or "The Power to Save the Fallen" Part 2, digital edition, November 27, 1997, by Holiness Data Ministry.

3. Her story is recorded in the first three gospels of the New Testament: Matthew 9:20-22; Mark 5:25-34; Luke 8:43-48.

CHAPTER 5

1. Kim Painter, "Loneliness takes its toll," usatoday.com, April 23, 2006, http://www.usatoday.com/news/health/2006-04-23-loneliness_x.htm, accessed October 11, 2012.

2. A. A. Milne and Ernest H. Shepard, *Winnie-the-Pooh* (New York: Dutton, 1926, 1961).

3. Gilbert Bilzekian, *Community 101* (location 849).

4. Mary Stewart van Leeuwen, *Gender and Grace: Women and Men in a Changing World* (Leicester: Inter-Varsity Press, 1990), 228.

5. Dietrich Bonhoeffer, Geffrey B. Kelly, Daniel W. Bloesch, and James H. Burtness, *Life Together; Prayerbook of the Bible* (Minneapolis: Fortress Press, 1996), 38.

6. Richard J. Foster, *Celebration of Discipline: the Path to Spiritual Growth* (San Francisco: Harper & Row, 1978), 113.

7. Anne Jackson, *Permission to Speak Freely: Essays and Art on Fear, Confession, and Grace* (Nashville: Thomas Nelson, 2010), 147.

CHAPTER 6

1. This metaphor was originally used in a lecture by Dr. Morris Weigelt in 2010.

2. John Donne, "Holy Sonnet XIV," public domain.

3. Definition from a lecture by Dr. Michael Cook on January 11, 2011, at Huntington University.

4. Gerald L. Sittser, *Water from a Deep Well: Christian Spirituality from Early Martyrs to Modern Missionaries* (Downers Grove, Ill.: IVP Books, 2007).

5. Wayne Cordeiro, *The Divine Mentor* (Bloomington, Minn.: Bethany House, 2007).

6. Among others, I recommend *The Spirit of the Disciplines* by Dallas Willard, *Celebration of Discipline* by Richard Foster, and *The Upward Call* by Wesley D. Tracy, E. Dee Freeborn, Janine Tartaglia, and Morris A. Weigelt.

CHAPTER 7

1. Therese Martin, *Story of a Soul: The Autobiography of St. Therese of Lisieux*, 3rd ed., trans. John Clarke (Washington, D.C.: ICS Publications, 1996), 208.

2. Nehemiah 1.

3. David Wilkerson, "A Call to Anguish," sermon at Times Square Church (New York: September 2002).

4. For a more complete examination of this passage and others, I found this book by Craig S. Keener particularly helpful: *Paul, Women, and Wives: Marriage and Women's Ministry in the Letters of Paul* (Peabody, Mass.: Hendrickson, 1992).

5. Scott Thumma and Warren Bird, *The Other 80 Percent: Turning Your Church's Spectators into Active Participants* (San Francisco: Jossey-Bass, 2011), xxi-xxii.

6. Brother Lawrence, *The Practice of the Presence of God* (New Kensington, Pa.: Whitaker House, 1982), 80-81.

7. Martin, *Story of a Soul*, 194.